**I WAS NEVER ALONE
OR
*OPORNIKI***

I WAS NEVER ALONE

OR *OPORNIKI*

AN ETHNOGRAPHIC PLAY ON
DISABILITY IN RUSSIA

CASSANDRA HARTBLAY

Teaching Culture: Ethnographies for the Classroom

UNIVERSITY OF TORONTO PRESS
Toronto Buffalo London

© University of Toronto Press 2020
Toronto Buffalo London
utorontopress.com
Printed and bound by CPI Group (UK) Ltd, Croydon, CR0 4YY

ISBN 978-1-4875-8841-0 (cloth)   ISBN 978-1-4875-8842-7 (EPUB)
ISBN 978-1-4875-8840-3 (paper)   ISBN 978-1-4875-8843-4 (PDF)

Library and Archives Canada Cataloguing in Publication

Title: I was never alone or oporniki: An ethnographic play on disability in Russia /
    Cassandra Hartblay.
Names: Hartblay, Cassandra, 1984– author.
Series: Teaching culture.
Description: Series statement: Teaching culture: ethnographies for the classroom |
    Includes bibliographical references and index.
Identifiers: Canadiana (print) 20200281119 | Canadiana (ebook) 20200281232 | ISBN
    9781487588410 (cloth) | ISBN 9781487588403 (paper) | ISBN 9781487588427
    (EPUB) | ISBN 9781487588434 (PDF)
Subjects: LCSH: People with disabilities – Russia (Federation) – Drama.
Classification: LCC PS3608.A78715967 I5 2020 | DDC 812/.6–dc23

We welcome comments and suggestions regarding any aspect of our publications—
please feel free to contact us at news@utorontopress.com or visit us at
utorontopress.com.

University of Toronto Press acknowledges the financial assistance to its publishing
program of the Canada Council for the Arts and the Ontario Arts Council, an agency
of the Government of Ontario.

Canada Council   Conseil des Arts
for the Arts   du Canada

ONTARIO ARTS COUNCIL
CONSEIL DES ARTS DE L'ONTARIO
an Ontario government agency
un organisme du gouvernement de l'Ontario

Funded by the   Financé par le
Government   gouvernement
of Canada   du Canada

Contents

Ethnographer's Essay

Appendixes

Acknowledgments

This project was made possible through support from several institutions, and would not have come into being without the grace, patience, generosity, and participation of many people and communities.

My years working at CEC ArtsLink prepared me to arrive in Russia as an ethnographer from abroad already with a grasp of cultural currents and trends in the arts in Russia.

My graduate studies at UNC-Chapel Hill profoundly shaped the research and my understanding of what is possible. Especially, I am grateful to Renee Alexander Craft and Joseph Megel in Performance Studies for offering me the tools to move from ethnography to theater and my comrades in those courses. The faculty in the anthropology department nurtured my scholarship and made space for this project to move forward and celebrated its creation alongside my dissertation based on the same fieldwork. Especially, I am grateful to Michele Rivkin-Fish, Jocelyn Chua, Arturo Escobar, the now-departed Dottie Holland and Bill Lachicotte, and then-chair Rudi Colleredo-Mansfeld. The Moral Economies of Medicine Working Group (particularly Peter Redfield and Sue Estroff), medical humanities, and Arts at the Core (especially Jane Thrailkill) supported the play in its early phases of development. The Center for Slavic, Eurasian, and East European Studies offered me community as an early-career graduate student. The Carolina Seminar on Russia and Its Empires created an intellectual environment in which to ask critical questions about the representation and historiography of

Russia in anglophone popular and scholarly discourse. Jehanne Gheith at Duke University supported the project through several iterations. I'm grateful to the fellow travelers who in one way or another entered my orbits during my time as a graduate student at UNC and were part of the creative world that made this work possible, including Pavithra Vasudevan, Katie Akin, Sara Juengst, Lindsey Wallace, Adam Leeds, Stevie Larson, Diana Gomez-Correal, Marie Garlock, Aaron Hale-Dorrell, and many others. I am grateful to Joy Weeber, Ellen Perry, Cuquis Robledo, and other disability advocates in North Carolina for holding space for this project and its possible contributions, and for important feedback along the way.

This project became fully possible thanks to the support that I received as a postdoctoral scholar at UC San Diego in the Collaboratory for Ethnographic Design (CoLED), 2015–17. I am deeply grateful to that community for offering a foundation from which to take risks with ethnographic outputs. The Collaboratory was a mirage of a project, a kind of ephemeral collaboration between ethnographers interested in thinking about the design of ethnography and the ethnography of design across geographically dispersed UC campuses. For the opportunity to experience this fleeting incubator for ethnographic creativity, I am thankful to its many members and participants, and those who launched the project: Elana Zilberg, Julie Burelle, Joe Hankins, Keith Murphy, George Marcus, Roshi Khesti, Christo Sims, Lilly Irani, Cristiana Giordano, Saiba Varma, Nancy Postero, Joe Dumit, Lissa Caldwell, and many more. Yelena Gluzman and Christina Aushana were fabulous comrades and shockworkers in conference and workshop execution. If *I Was Never Alone* arrived in San Diego in 2015 as a script draft, the CoLED postdoc offered me the time and space to revise it into a fully realized script (many sunny afternoons in Trolley Barn Park with the dog and sunlight dappled through eucalyptus trees were passed making edits after table readings). The real possibility to take the script from ethnographic experiment to theatrical process was made possible by the phenomenal support of a New Frontiers grant from UC San Diego to pursue this work as an interdisciplinary project. I am thankful to Deborah Stein for asking me questions about what the script does dramatically that I have continued to think through and grapple with both in the accompanying essay in this volume and in my plans for the future of the project.

I am deeply grateful to an amazing cohort of theater students, professionals, and actors who in 2016 staged the play at the Shank Theatre in the UC San Diego Jacobs Theatre District/La Jolla Playhouse. That workshop continues to hold a special place in my memory as a moment when this project benefitted from bringing ethnographers, disability studies scholars, and theater practitioners together in space and time. I am especially grateful to Julie Burelle for her support in facilitating the project and her dramaturgy during the workshop. The UC San Diego disability studies community has shaped me in ways that I am still only now discovering, and I imagine will continue to impact my work for years to come: Patrick Anderson, David Serlin, Carol Padden, Brian Goldberg, then-fellow postdoc Mara Green, and many more. The project could never have happened without the support of business officer Gayle Aruta and then-chair Val Hartouni in the Department of Communication, and the immense patience of the liaisons between the UCSD theater department and the La Jolla Playhouse (while the two entities share space, the dynamics of usage were quite complicated). The union professionals who executed the technical elements of the staged workshop were immovably excellent. I am particularly grateful to my dear collaborator, the reason I took a chance on San Diego, Louise Hickman. And, I continue to be thankful to Jason and Laura Dorwart for the incredible energy, passion, and political resolve that they brought to this project; I continue to be inspired by their disability advocacy and scholarship, and the trajectory of *I Was Never Alone* is deeply, deeply due to their extraordinary expertise in disability theater. I am grateful to all of the actors and crew who participated in the San Diego staging and made this script into a play.

Looking back at my time at Yale University, I'm struck by the incredible generosity of the scholars across campus who took the time to encourage me and nurture this project. My postdoctoral position there was hosted by a very welcoming team in Russian studies at the MacMillan Center for Area Studies, and the administrative and academic overseers of my disciplinary cross-appointment in anthropology. I was lucky to have the mentorship of Doug Rogers, who seemed to make anything I could dream up seem possible while somehow always remaining calm. I am also grateful for the support of the Slavic studies community, including John McKay and Marijeta Bozovic (whose vision for the future of Slavic studies is a bright light – and I am a disciple). Elise Morrison in theater studies took a chance on creative collaboration with an unknown postdoc and directed a staged reading of *I Was Never Alone*, an act of artistic bravery and vulnerability for which I will always be grateful. I hold close to my heart the junior faculty who became comrades whose companionship buoyed me through the New Haven winter that year, especially Jess Newman, Eda Pepi, and Greta LaFleur. This project was also deeply shaped by Kate Dudley and the Working Group on Ethnography and Oral History at Yale. The group workshopped the format for this volume and in many ways sent me back to the drawing board in regards to what the elements accompanying the script itself might be and do.

The symposium committee of Soyuz, the research network for postsocialist cultural studies (of both the American Anthropological Association and the Association for Slavic, Eastern European, and Eurasian Studies), made space in the program for a staged reading of *I Was Never Alone*, structuring the 2018 symposium theme around performance. For this, I am particularly grateful to Larisa Kurtovic and Tatiana Chudakova (whose respective terms as president the project spanned), Martha Lampland (who came up with the crazy idea to stage the play at a Soyuz Symposium), the then-programming coordinator Emily Channell-Justice, to Doug Rogers for suggesting that we host the symposium at Yale and pulling it all together, and to Alana Lemon, who gave the symposium's keynote address.

In 2018, Ilya Utekhin, Anna Klepikova, Masha Pirogovskaya, and Anna Altukhova at European University in Saint Petersburg organized the first staged reading of excerpts of the script in Russian. Numerous other anthropologists and Russianist colleagues have offered connections, ties, and suggestions. These possibilities are still in the works, and one day soon I hope to stage the work not only in North America but also in Russia. Each iteration offers new collaborators, and with them, wholly different theatrical results and different ethnographic insights.

This project, in its most basic conception, would not exist without the many colleagues who have made it possible to think critically about disability in the former Soviet Union. These include Anastasia Kayiatos, Fran Bernstein and Eliot Borenstein, Katerina Kolářová and Kathi Wiedlack, Elena Iarskaia-Smirnova (and the late Pavel

Romanov), Sarah Phillips, Michael Rasell, Sasha Kondakov, and many others. I am also deeply grateful to the overlapping cohorts of scholars affiliated with the Disability Research Interest Group of the American Anthropological Association and the Society for Disability Studies, especially those who have championed this research in one way or another, including Devva Kasnitz, Karen Nakamura, Faye Ginsburg, Rayna Rapp, Pam Block, Michele Friedner, Zoe Wool, Christine Sargent, and many others.

The current iteration of this book came about in part through invited talks at a variety of institutions, and I am grateful to Krista Harper and Julie Hemment at UMASS, Magdalena Kazubowski-Houston at York University, Richard Grinker and Anthropocinema at GWU, Kristin Bright at Middlebury, and others for organizing those opportunities and supporting this work.

I am grateful to my collaborators and queer/crip coconspirators in the interinstitutional Critical Design Lab, including Aimi Hamraie, Kevin Gotkin, Jarah Moesch, Leah Samples, and the others who have nudged me along through monthly virtual check-ins as this project has evolved over the past three years, and for believing in the iterative, nonnormative, and speculative potential of this work.

I am grateful to my colleagues and students in the Department of Anthropology, the Interdisciplinary Centre for Health and Society, Slavic Languages and Literatures, disability studies, and Centre for European, Russian, and Eurasian Studies at the University of Toronto.

I am grateful to anonymous reviewers of this text who suggested alternate translations, pointed out concerns, and challenged me to make this text compelling to a variety of audiences. And, I have been so lucky to work with the editors and staff at the University of Toronto Press, especially Anne Brackenbury, who brought me on board, and Carli Hansen, who ferried the book to completion.

This project would not have come to be without Jude Wobst, whose enduring perseverance made learning Russian as a public high school student a possibility long after the Cold War initiative that started high school Russian language programs had faded to a memory elsewhere. *Spasibo*!

Prior to and long after all of this, I am grateful to my family and friends. None of this would be possible without my many theater, performance, and artistic mentors and collaborators over the years, too many to name here. My father, Scott Roman Hartblay, instilled in me a sense of reading and writing as a practice around which one might organize one's life and taught me that living itself is one big magical mystery tour. My mother, Marian Hartblay, holds creativity and a sense of wonder as the flame that gathers her household together. The members of our blended family, especially Migle V. Hartblay and Andrew Glace, have supports me in my travels, study, politics, artistic and intellectual pursuits, and shaped this journey in innumerable ways. And to my loves, you know who you are.

I continue to be in awe of the profound generosity, bravery, and vulnerability of my coperformers-collaborators-interlocutors whose stories make up this project. This work is for you.

Foreword: The Play's the Thing

The last thirty years have been a seminal period of critique, rethinking, and experimentation with anthropology's sustaining genre form – the ethnography. A key concern of this activity has been to create texts that enliven dialogue between ethnographer/subject/audience, and in so doing challenge the traditional authority of texts. In place of one authorial voice, we have sought forms for ethnography that offer polyphonic representation, wherein informants are not paraphrased but speak for themselves (see Clifford and Marcus 2010). In the 1980s, inspired by Bakhtin and other, especially feminist, thinkers, there was hope for the multi- or co-authored experiment in writing. There were a few, and some notable, exemplars of ethnographic texts written in dialogic form, that is, in a manner that shared the authorial voice between ethnographer and ethnographic subjects. Since that moment, ethnography, though considerably expanded in its narrative and analytic imaginaries, has largely remained in its textual monologic tradition (that is, giving primacy to the voice of the ethnographer). Yet, during that same period, there were alternatives on the margins, including pioneering theater anthropology – Conquergood, the Turners, Fabian, among others – and the steady development of ethnographic film and media beyond strictly observational commitments. A coalescence of these working traditions brings into view a different "post" moment than the one we imagined in the late twentieth century. Hartblay's work, for one, shows us, definitively, that we have arrived at such a moment.

Nothing did, and still nothing has (and perhaps nothing should have?) shaken the *rite-de-passage* of the observational fieldwork project – leading to the genre ethnography with experimental moves within limits – as the *entre* into anthropological careers. Yet, in this volume, Hartblay's account of her parallel development as theater/ performance artist and first-project anthropologist makes for extraordinarily valuable and absorbing reading, more so in that we have arrived at a time when discussions of alternative ("multi-modal") forms for producing career qualifying ethnographic research are under lively discussion.

Hartblay's contribution here shows that the formal modes of professional reception of ethnographic research in anthropology – responding to the textual artifacts of research – are enhanced by other episodes, acts, studios, para-sites, third spaces of reception, response, and commentary to authoritative, analytic argument from fieldwork in the making. This is what the contemporary development of performance/theater anthropology offers – though without any certainty that such a venture as Hartblay develops here ever "docks" back in academic debate according to the latter's authority. With suspenseful uncertainty, the script inventions of Hartblay and their development out of what began as canonical ethnographic research moves in exciting directions of its own through theatrical production. Where fieldwork realized in theater projects eventually intersects with the demands of ethnographic analytics is an exciting and suspenseful dimension of Hartblay's work in motion.

This work demonstrates and articulates brilliantly how different ways of working, defining ethnographic projects, evolve from the still canonical fieldwork project. Having produced an ethnographic dissertation from fieldwork, with a promissory of written ethnography in the future, Hartblay first creates this extraordinary volume of performance/theater ethnography, seeding into it a vivid account of her engagements with Russia, its language, recent history, and cultural understandings of disability – all told through the experience of the disabled interlocutors entangled in a society bound to mistake them. In so doing, she deeply involves the reader in performance, dialogue, and polyphony, all the while feeding the contexts of fieldwork and ethnography into her presentation and commentary on the script.

Hartblay is deeply in artistic and writerly control of the shaping of her own unique text, and me saying more in the manner of a "foreword" will only get in the way of a clear strategy of presentation (beginning with a brief "Note from the Ethnographer") and a remarkable essay, with a set of diverse but extraordinarily valuable appendixes (including one that expertly shows how any teacher or instructor might integrate performative, theatrical elements practically into a variety of classroom/seminar situations).

However, I have perhaps one helpful suggestion for the reader about to set out on the carefully organized, absorbing course that Hartblay has set for us. It makes complete sense, and is perhaps the convention, to open with/expose the reader first to the playscript, followed by photos, before launching into an essay that is foreword, introduction, extended critical essay, and practical guide all in one. However, as with many others I know, I am a problematic reader of play transcripts – the magic for me is only in the live performance. While I was easily absorbed in reading the introductory account/ short monograph that follows the script, I struggled to follow the dialogue of the play with reading alone. Going back to the script following the other sections of the book and watching the performances, I had more to work with. For instance, revisiting the script with Hartblay's explanation of the Russian concept of *oporniki* in mind, I read the interactions between characters differently.

Watching performances brought me closer to the sensory power of polyphonic ethnography that has generated such a brilliantly designed and explained project. I recommend readers encountering this text for the first time to perform or view performances of the text to enliven the script's dynamic potential.

So as a de facto contemporary historian of anthropological textuality, with a longing for performative dimensions of the stuff of ethnographic research that the printed page only can incompletely satisfy, *I Was Never Alone or Oporniki* is a challenging, absorbing breakthrough.

George E. Marcus, University of California, Irvine
co-editor, *Writing Culture* (1986)
co-author, *Designs for an Anthropology of the Contemporary* (2008)
co-author, *Ethnography by Design: Scenographic Experiments in Fieldwork* (2019)

About This Book: A Note from the Ethnographer

This book is arranged around the script of a play, titled *I Was Never Alone or Oporniki*. While the book contains several supplementary elements (a reflective essay, discussion of the method used to create the script, and appendices addressing readers in a variety of disciplines and career stages), the play itself, as George Marcus notes in the foreword, is indeed "the thing," that is, the centerpoint of the volume and the impetus for its existence. I encourage readers to read the work aloud, perform scenes, and create or attend a live staging of the play. Readers may find it useful to supplement their reading of the text of the play by watching video clips or engaging other sensory media from past live performances, available on the companion website to this book (www.iwasneveralone.org). Appendix 4 offers suggestions for reading this book in a classroom setting.

I Was Never Alone is based on ethnographic research in a regional city in Northwest Russia (2010–14). I adapted each of the "portraits" in the script from transcripts of interviews that I conducted, in Russian, with adults with disabilities in the city. The people represented in the script have disabilities related to physical impairments that affect their movement, as the Russian word *oporniki* in the title indicates.[*] In this sense, this work cannot be considered representative of the

---

[*] For a further discussion of *oporniki*, see the section of the essay that follows the script titled "We Were Never Alone: Words for Disability."

broader array of embodied conditions that are considered to be disabilities; Deaf and Blind communities, or those with intellectual or mental disabilities, are not present in this script.

I have arranged the play as a series of portraits – some of these are nearly monologues, but in all cases, there are some interactions with other on- or off-stage characters. In most cases, I have knit together text from multiple interviews, or condensed text from a single interview to create a coherent narrative of a performable length. The text that you will find here is therefore not strictly a verbatim reproduction of my interview transcripts, but nearly so. The most significant change from the original interview transcripts (aside from the translation from Russian) is that I have removed the questions that I posed as the interviewer: there is no "ethnographer" character in the scene per se. Instead, the audience performs the role of interviewer. Except when addressing other characters in the scene, the actors speak directly to the audience, as if the audience collectively were conducting the interview.

The script may be read as a work of ethnography, as a kind of collection of condensed oral history interviews in translation, or as a script for performance. Anthropologists, Russian studies readers, disability studies scholars and activists, theater practitioners, and students with any of these interests will be drawn to rather different elements of the script itself and the accompanying material. I therefore invite the reader to simply skip over those elements of this volume that are uninteresting or obvious; one challenge of composing a text for interdisciplinary audiences is that no one version will please everyone.

There are a few more points that may be useful to consider before delving into the script. First, I consider this work as a companion to a theoretical work that takes the form of a traditional academic ethnographic monograph (extending from my dissertation research); selections from this work are also published as stand-alone articles, which may make useful supplementary reading for some audiences. But, the play can be read either in conversation with those works or as a stand-alone piece. As often happens when ethnographers work between several publications at once, certain segments of text will be recognizably repeated between the play and the academic writing.

Ethnographers will likely be curious as to the methodological and ethical considerations and mode of working behind this work. I address these questions further in the essay following the script, but it may be useful to have in mind as you read that the real people whose words have been adapted to create these portraits all consented to be interviewed and participate in ethnographic research about the lives of people with disabilities in their city. Some of the people represented here are close friends, with whom I shared many experiences and recorded multiple interviews. Others are people whom I had only met two or three times in person when I first drafted the script, but with whom I shared a broad network of mutual acquaintances to the extent that they were comfortable opening their lives to me in the course of a single interview. As the project has developed, I returned to the field site with the script (rendered in Russian) and workshopped it with the people on whom the characters are based (a process discussed further in the essay following the script).

While the play is largely a verbatim adaptation of my interview transcripts, artistic license of course played a role in the creation of this work. In certain places, I have summed up a great deal of dialogue with a paraphrased line, or inserted a sentence or two to contextualize a statement. But overall, my intention has been to preserve the actual words of the interviewee. Similarly, I have sometimes retained the actual location in which an interview took place as the suggested setting in the staging; in other cases, I have changed the implied location slightly, or selected a location other than the one where the interview from which the majority of the monologue is drawn took place. I have done so in order to best capture some element of each character's life in the format of a short portrait.

I myself am an American and a native English speaker. I speak and comprehend Russian fluently, but with an accent and without the full command of a native speaker. All of the interviews for this project were conducted in Russian. A few of the interviewees for this project knew some English, but we never spoke English together. At times, my status as a foreigner and non-native speaker actually helped me to solicit detailed explanations of ideas or concepts that a native speaker might have been expected to already comprehend. I also do not currently identify as a person with a disability, although I have been a member of disability communities since childhood. In this sense, while I present to my interlocutors as able-bodied, and therefore do not share a specific embodied experience, I was easily identified as an ally and (to a degree) an insider in disability culture; I was already acquainted with the vocabularies, problems, and general contours of ableism and inaccess which I asked my interlocutors to tell me about, both in Russia and abroad. Both my interlocutors and I were curious about the question of whether there is a global disability culture – in the sense of shared experiences and commitments – and where the needs, goals, and experiences of people living in different sociopolitical, environmental, and geographic contexts differ.

Translation is always a tricky business. The words of certain narrators represented here – who use unusual combinations of words or speak with unusual cadences and attitudes – have presented a challenge to translate. I have tried to capture the nuance, register, and style of speech of each of the characters, but inevitably there are places where a bilingual reader would disagree with my rendition.

I have, throughout the script, provided Russian words scattered in the English text, which an actor may choose to include for emphasis and a dash of "Russianness." I have provided in the text both the transliterated Russian word or name (Russian is usually written in the Cyrillic alphabet) and, in brackets, an approximation of the Russian manner of pronunciation, with the stressed syllable in all caps. I have provided a list of Russian words by scene in Appendix 8. In certain scenes, characters have side conversations – phone calls or exchanges with passing characters – which could be performed either in Russian or English, depending on the preference of the production. As a result, in several cases I have provided both the Russian and English for these exchanges. Some information about the character's social world is lost on non-Russian speakers by performing these exchanges in Russian; on the other hand, it is an opportunity to incorporate Russian into the performance and might tickle Russian-speakers in the audience. Russian language words throughout this book are romanized according to a modified BGN/PCGN system, to prioritize accessibility for non-Russian-speaking anglophone readers.

Script

Production History

I Was Never Alone was first developed as a play in a performance studies playwriting seminar in 2015 at UNC-Chapel Hill; early experiments with this format of research and performance were developed in Renee Alexander Craft's performance ethnography methods seminars. The work also had two process readings at UNC-CH in 2015 and 2016. For a staged reading in February 2016, Joseph Megel directed, Ariana Rivens stage-managed, and Joseph Amodei designed lighting and projection. Actors included Ash Heffernan as Vera, Cuquis Robledo as Alina, George Barrett as Rudak, and Meredith Kemple as Anya. In early 2016, the project was awarded a Frontiers of Innovation Scholars Program (FISP) grant from the University of California at San Diego (UCSD). Script development continued at UCSD, with project mentors Deborah Stein and Elana Zilberg, and input from Julie Burelle as well as collaborators and research participants in Russia. In the summer of 2016, the people whose stories are represented in the work participated in a process reading of a Russian-language version of the script in person. The UCSD grant culminated in a two-week workshop and process production on 7 and 8 October 2016 at the Shank Theatre in UCSD's Jacobs Theatre District with support from the Vice Chancellor's Office for Equity, Diversity, and Inclusion and the Department of Communication. Joseph Megel directed; Bryan P. Clements was the production stage manager; Julie Burelle was the dramaturg; Jason Dorwart was assistant director; Joel Britt and Charlie

Jicha designed lights and set respectively. Louise Hickman designed the disability access schema for the performances. Vladimir Rudak performed live musical accompaniment. The play was performed in a staged reading at Yale University in the spring of 2018, as part of the annual symposium of Soyuz, the research interest group for Postsocialist Cultural Studies of the American Anthropological Association and the Association for Slavic, Eurasian, and Eastern European Studies. Elise Morrison directed; Rachel Chew designed projections; Dana Smooke designed lighting; Chayton Pabich designed sound; and Yuki Hayasaka was production assistant. Actors included Shannon DeVido as Vera; Sommer Carbuccia as Vakas; Caitlin Wells as Alina; Patrick Tombs as Sergei; and Abbey Burgess as Anya. The first performative reading of excerpts from the work in Russian was held at the European University in Saint Petersburg in October 2018.

Cast of Characters

VERA

A woman in her early thirties. Young and stereotypically good looking. Keeps her hair in a shiny, cherry red bob. Busy mom of two. Married for a second time; her husband is a "Real Russian Man" type – big and tough on the outside, soft on the inside. Vera uses a wheelchair since an accident when she was a young teenager – she is paralyzed from the waist down. Socially adept. Aware of appearances. A little bit of a party girl in her younger days.

VAKAS

Early thirties. Ladies' man. Big eyes, shy smile. Likes poetry, or anything else about love. Walks with a shuffle and poor balance. Traumatic brain injury survivor after being hit by a car as a child. Due to his injury, he speaks very slowly, in a labored slow drawl. Because each phrase takes him so long to pronounce, he often has to pause to breathe at unexpected points in a sentence. Ordinarily, he dislikes speaking in public and is self-conscious about his speech impairment. Likes pretty girls, his desktop computer, and digital photography. Lives with his younger brother and his parents, in the family apartment, where Vakas spends most of his days.

ALINA

A thirty-something-year-old woman. Loves the spotlight, has trouble speaking loudly. Pretty long dark hair, big dark eyes, killer cheekbones, doesn't like to brush her teeth. Has cerebral palsy, uses a wheelchair. Low dexterity in her arms, so relies on others to push her, help her dress. Her favorite colors are red and pink; she frequently wears both, in combination. She spends most of her time with her mom, a retired school janitor, in their apartment. Alina is not afraid to state her opinion.

SERGEI

A man in his early thirties. The quiet, respectable type. Likes to sing soulful folk songs, watch war movies with masculine sentimentality. Born with cerebral palsy, he walks independently, but with difficulty. He doesn't use crutches or other aides, but he also avoids walking long distances. Slow to produce an opinion, even-tempered. Tries to do the right thing. Does piecemeal video editing and graphic design work from his computer at home, mostly passed on through family and friends. Lives with his parents, who both work full time. Mama's boy.

RUDAK

Forty-something man. Local celebrity. Lead singer and guitarist in a popular local rock band. Likes to wear a crocheted skullcap when he performs. Writes, edits, and shoots documentary films with a creative collaborator in Petrozavodsk. His narrative films, written and produced with fellow *spinal'niki* in Moscow, have been shown in international disability film festivals. Uses a wheelchair after a spinal injury. Receives a disability pension, works from home on creative projects. Shares an apartment with his mom, and sometimes his nieces and nephews. Unmarried (officially). Kind, mischievous, and creative.

ANYA

Mid-thirties professional. Favors striped blouses, fine jewelry. Works as a psychologist and social worker, specializing in disabilities and social perceptions of self. The only character who uses a power wheelchair. Has a progressive muscular disorder. She moves slowly, finds many common objects heavy to lift, needs help to roll over, sit up, open her flip phone. Lives in an apartment that she shares with her caretaker (whom she pays with her disability stipend, using her earned income to live on). Her parents live in another building a few doors down. Leads with her sharp intellect and wry sense of humor. Later reveals her disarming emotional intelligence. A sympathetic listener and a good flirt. Quiet voice, loud opinions.

WAITER/WAITRESS
A young person wearing a half apron, a button-down shirt, and jeans.

MAMA
A working-class woman in her sixties with short gray hair.

TRUMPET PLAYER, BASSIST (OPT: DRUMMER, GUITARIST)
Men in their late thirties or early forties.

LARISSA
A woman in her twenties.

Setting

Various family homes and cafés in a small city in Northwest Russia.

Time

Set in the year 2012 or 2013.

Note

Russian words in the script are marked in bolded italics. For less familiar words, a pronunciation is offered in brackets. The words are also listed in a pronunciation and definition guide at the end of this volume (Appendix 8, beginning on page 193). A slash (/) indicates where the next speech begins.

Portrait I

VERA

Vera wheels her way into a space in a manual wheelchair, approaches a table, pulls out a chair from one side of the table, and sets it aside. She backs up and pulls in a few times to situate herself at a table. The table is set in a manner befitting a not very formal but not too cheap local Russian café. There is a napkin holder on the table of the type that displays paper napkins in a fan of triangles, salt and pepper shakers, and a pair of menus in large portfolio menu holders. A glass case with an assortment of Russian and "French" pastries is visible behind her, lined with several boxes of "Ahmad" brand tea in a variety of flavors. Once settled, she unzips her fitted blue leather jacket and unwinds a long narrow black knitted scarf. Removing a knit black ski cap with a rhinestone decal, she tucks it beside her on the seat of her wheelchair, smooths her sleek, bright red bob, and presses her freshly glossed lips. She speaks quickly, easily, confidently, in the manner of a popular girl who isn't sure about what she thinks of the person she's talking to.

VERA: Well, so let's start from the beginning then, like, when I was born, I didn't have a disability. When I was ten I had a spinal injury. So, then, from ten on I was in a wheelchair, *v koliaske [vVff-kol-YAWs-kyeh].*

It was a long time ago, sort of. How long –

(eyes wide, realizing how many years)

Twenty years or so!

WAITER: *Chto budete? [Sh-TOE BOO-dyeh-tyeh]* What'll you have?

VERA: *(looks down at the menu and thinks for a moment, then, pointing to the menu)*

You don't have any cherry ones? I'll have the apple one. And regular tea. Two sugars, no milk.

Sooo.

(launches into a story, speaking quickly, trying to get the story out)

I started out going to a regular school – well, until the second grade. So then, in the second grade, I got injured. And after the second grade, they – they moved me to home education. That means that in school I – I graduated high school by studying at home. So, like most of the kids, probably, who have –

(gestures, as if to say, you know, disability)

So. The thing is that, hmm, at home they give you fewer hours of instruction, and then it's more difficult to apply to go on to college.

So. Um. Well – I got in anyway, I applied to – in Russia the law says that the disabled – *invalidi [een-vawl-LEED-dee]*[1] – don't apply like everyone else, we just take exams. So I did my exam and applied. I got in and went – I can't remember – they changed the name of the institution!

(laughs; starts to enjoy herself)

So, ummm – I graduated with a degree in early childhood education. Well, like, I graduated, but I didn't go start working. Because, when I was still working on my degree, I realized that I shouldn't work with children, that I wouldn't, because I get so fricking impatient with them!

(smiles)

I just get fed up, because children can be – really awful! Because ... like, well ... it just doesn't work out for me, I don't have enough patience.

---

1 For a discussion of the variegation of English and Russian language terminology for discussing disability, see Appendix 2. For a full pronunciation guide to Russian language words in the script, see Appendix 8.

(smiles)

Or something.

(checks the screen on the front of her flip phone)

Sooo. Then after that, I went to get a degree in economics,
as a bookkeeper-accountant. Well, wait – after my first
degree I didn't work, but, while I was finishing my first
degree, in my last year, I gave birth to my son.

So, that was also sort of hard, and so I thought for a long
time, weighing my options, weighing my options. So
then I was thinking – because I get really bored just living
day after day, I decided to go back to school.

(smiling)

Sooo. Well, then everything more or less worked out okay,
because somewhere around six months after I started,
Svetlana [Sveat-LAHN-nah] got me a job working on
this social work project, and – Well, then I was more or
less employed. And in terms of money, they started to
pay me little by little.

(trails off, then begins anew)

And everything more or less worked out.

(pause)

Then, well, when my son was three, my husband was in
an accident and died. So. And we were left alone, just
the two of us. Well, the two of us, but we still had my
parents.

*(WAITER places a teacup and saucer on the table sitting on a napkin
that is sitting on a matching saucer in front of her. Next to it, the
WAITER places another matching plate, on which is another napkin,
two cubes of white sugar, and a very small teaspoon)*

So then there's my parents, and me and **Igor [EE-gore]**. Well
and then – that era passed. And then in 2009 I – um – I
met –

(server arrives with a pastry on a plate, and places it on the table)

my husband, the second one.

His name is **Andrei**. So. In, like, the end of 2009, we had a
wedding, and like, now we also have a daughter, she is

already 18 months, almost. So there's that. Well, that's the
short version.

*(VERA's phone rings – a rock song – she opens the flip phone and
answers)*

Yes, Igor.

*(listens to her son for about ten seconds, then both patiently and trying
to quickly get off the phone)*

She's not here. I'm not with **babushka** ... Well wait ten
minutes, and see, she'll be back, okay? ... Okay.

(closes phone; speaks to the audience)

It's just that I left the two kids at home. So – my son – he's a
little –

(laughs)

He's already pretty grown-up, nine years old, but still, he's
still pretty little to be alone with the baby.

(Pauses. Then – chattering at a quick pace again ...)

So, the thing is – my first job – my role there was to – what's
the right way to put it? Hold on, I'll remember.

(to herself)

What was it? "Trainer for youth groups." So like, when
people with disabilities share,

(reciting)

when they share their own experiences with other people
with disabilities, then like, it helps, sort of, to address
social and psychological problems they might have in
common.

Now I have a job, online, I work with a **Petersburg** firm.
I've been working there about, three, or maybe four
years. So that work is really technical. But, since the pay
is good –

(laughs, modestly)

And, also at the same time I work on other things too. I
don't want to go to school any more myself, but I write
essays and term papers for college students. So, I help the
cheaters get through school. Or something like that. But
generally –

(VERA's phone rings again; she opens it)

Da, Igor ... Yes ... In the cupboard ... Just sit tight for a few
   minutes ... Okay ... Okay. All right.

*(VERA hangs up, sighs, sets her phone down. Then, as if responding
to a question from the audience about her memories about when she
became disabled)*

The kind of memories, you mean my feelings after the
   accident? There really weren't any at all. Totally nothing.
   I – I was in touch with a lot of kids that had become
   disabled who were older than me. They were twenty or
   thirty. So, for them, it was really a tragedy. For them life
   completely changed, that life was completely broken.
   Since I was still a child, really, I – I didn't feel like a major
   tragedy had befallen me. Well, sure – when the girls
   were jumping rope or were doing gymnastics, of course
   there was that sting that I wanted to be doing it too. But,
   I wouldn't say that I was really *tormented* about it, even
   though it was upsetting, I wouldn't say *that* [meaning
   the suffering of emotional pain]. But – but I also have a
   mother who is – she's the kind of person that, like – she –

(imitating a mother speaking to a child)

"Don't start feeling sorry for yourself, don't say that you're
   a poor unlucky little baby." No. And she only ever got
   upset on the balcony, she always hid it, which is hard to
   do at home, she did whatever was necessary to pull it off.
   Sooo.

(quietly, thoughtfully)

The thing is, like, parents probably play a big role. So.

Even though I get along with my mom, there are a lot
   of people who get stuck living with their parents and
   can't have a personal life. But not with us. With my first
   husband – we – we met umm, there was an evening
   event for people with disabilities to hang out, and we
   met there. So, then we dated for something like a year,
   probably? But my mom immediately liked him.

(imitating mom)

"He's good, he's so good, go, go, go!"

(not nearly as excited as the voice she used for her mom's reaction)

And it was like, well, okay, it could be good.

(VERA drinks from the teacup)

So. But my second husband, he's really something. He – he
has this personality – like a real tough guy. He was in
the army. So. And like my second husband even has a
disability. So – in the army, he was in **Chechnya**, enlisted,
and – he was shot there. He's really, a little – kind of
gruff. My mom, with him, it was hard for my mom with
him. My mom says, "Why don't you talk already – we're
over here, you're over there ... Are we just supposed to
split up the house between us?!" So, yeah.

Then I don't know what happened next. My friends, like
then I got to know my friends. I have, like now I have
this group, that I've found for myself, we have – two
other married couples. We would be friends anyway, and
there are even two couples, so it's like, we get together a
lot. And they have, we have, like, we're like a club – we
don't go out to bars,

(smiles)

because somehow at our age it's already not that great!
But like we just stay home a lot. But now like because of
the kids we don't have enough time.

*(As VERA trails off, she is looking down at her phone, thinking what
to say next. She picks it up quickly to answer just as it begins to ring
again)*

Da Igor ... Well ... No, what can you do, can you tell me?
Well, so play with her ... good, play, I'll come home soon,
I'll call Papa right now, I'll find out where he is ... doing
things, okay? I'm hanging up ... Yes, we're in different
places ...

(laughs)

Okay, my love! Bye! ... Kiss-kiss.

*(Hangs up the phone. Then, imitating her son, speaking to the
audience)*

"But, so papa's not with you? Are you for real in different
places?!? But where did papa GO?!"

(laughs, then as if responding to another question from the audience)

So many personal questions!!

(laughs, then indicating she will answer in a moment)

Just a second ...

(dials a pre-programmed number, then, to her husband)

Hi ...Where are you? ... Yep, okay ... No, no, not the one in the box. Get the liquid one. The one in the pink bottle? ... Right. That's it ... Okay, when you're ready.

(closes the flip phone and smiles at it for a moment, then again to the audience)

Okay! That's it! I've talked with the whole family!

(laughs; then, jokingly, to the audience)

Women, if you aren't married, don't do it! It's dark, they don't feed you well, and it's a lot of cleaning!

No, that's the dark view, of course – when like, my husband leaves on a business trip, I don't even come out to the café, I just relax! I have the whole house cleaned up, everything in its place, the dishes washed, everything else in order. Everything is perfect! *Vsyo Idial!* [*VIS-yo EE-dee-ahl*]

(then, in a dark voice)

My husband comes home, and it's "Vera, bring me something to eat! Vera, hand me the clicker! Vera, where is the charger?! Vera, where is the – ?!"

(laughs)

But actually, in terms of cooking, my husband is a very good cook.

(then, pausing, because she's set up a joke)

BUT, the way he cooks, it's like it cancels it out: he cooks for two hours, but then it takes three hours to clean the kitchen! Because the dishes will ALL be dirty! The kitchen will be a total mess! On the table, on the floors, on the walls, everywhere!

(laughs; then, although it's not quite true)

I *do* like to cook. But to tell you the truth, all the recipes that I post online, my husband will say that – what's that called, "It's just to show off to your friends on your wall, but, you won't make any of it!"

(giggles)

I don't usually spend time cooking, but then all of a sudden, I'll have time, and get inspired ... I *like* to do all the home things. So. But I don't get to do all of the things because – like, only sometimes when my daughter, falls asleep. Otherwise, you have to feed her and wash her and dress her fifty-seven times ...

(joking again)

Sometimes my friend calls me, and she says, "Are you home? I took my daughter to preschool, I cleaned up the house, and now I'm bored." And I say, "Now that's what I want – to have the time to be bored!"

It's so *nice* to just sit, to play some music or read the news! It's – it's hard to find time, it's too bad it almost never happens! It's as if you're doing things so that you don't have to do anything! It starts in the morning and goes all day long, every day, you go to bed, and then everything starts all over again ...

(sitting up straight, seeing her husband approaching through the window of the café, coming to pick her up. Then, with relief)

Oh, here comes Andrei!

Portrait II

VAKAS

Vakas is seated on a rolling desk chair, facing the audience. Several feet behind the desk chair is a large rectangular window, the interior of an eighth-floor 1980s-era Soviet apartment building with a winter sky beyond, hung with white crocheted curtains. Set facing a wall beside the window is a brown particleboard made-in-China computer desk, with a recent model PC, and a radio alarm clock on top. Set against the opposite wall is a fish tank, and a stationary bicycle. The room is very clean, and there are very few objects about. Vakas himself is wearing black sweatpants, a polo shirt, and a sweater. He has on black socks and an Adidas slide-on flip flop on one foot only. His blond hair is combed neatly, with a side part.

Vakas speaks very slowly, in a labored voice; line breaks indicate his irregular pattern of breathing midsentence.

VAKAS: So you heard
that i write
poems?
(waits for audience response)
Well?
(raises eyebrows in anticipation of an answer; then, gives up, starts anew, telling a story)
the fourteenth was the concert

that was really unusual, since i went out
yeah. but this – outing – makes me
feel something
but today i asked – it was beautiful –
let's go outside – he – Papa – didn't want to
that's what i live for – seeing people
art
getting to know someone brings me joy
it's hard – since i almost
don't go outside at all and my parents
keep me at home, keep an eye over the place and i don't like
    it and
i tell them so
but there's already been so much uproar
about this
when i was going to the store
so, i used to talk with the salesgirl there
and i liked that
and when i got out and would get out of the house, so to
    speak,
i would always show up at the store.
i found this really interesting salesgirl
it's in The Capitol shopping center
it has music – CDs.
i would go there often
a bunch of Sundays
it was always the same
salesgirl, and i liked her.
and one time when i
saw her i asked for
her to show me some things in
i wanted to give her
my book – the first one
but it was a different person
i asked where is *that* girl
and no one could tell me
i didn't even know her name
and i couldn't even leave the

book for her
the next Sunday i went back and
there standing there
was a different girl
i asked
where is she? she said, *what's her name?*
then, *i don't know who you mean*
and then the next week –
a different salesgirl
i wanted to give her my book and
i complimented her
these sorts of emotions
but i just liked her
how she looked
her face
i went every Sunday
and asked something
just to get to talk with someone
and obviously i shouldn't have
done that because
then she disappeared
and I wrote this poem
it was in my first book – the one I sent you

(Turns back to computer. Copies and pastes a poem, which appears on the screen, in Russian. VAKAS reads the text aloud, live or as a voiceover)

The Deity of My Love
I named a deity for you in my dream;
And it's true: that's what you've become to me!
And this world – suddenly – seems small
And these stars – my star has fallen
But with its fall
I offered my desire to the summer:
To love, to be feverishly aflame,
by this love, kept warm.
I just wish that at sunset
my destiny would come to me, washed out by rain;

And I would say, "Enough from me!
Become my goddess in waking life!"

БОЖЕСТВО МОЕЙ ЛЮБВИ

Я божеством во сне Тебя назвал;
И это правда: Ты для меня Им стала!
И этот мир – он для меня вдруг мал,
И звезды эти – моя звезда упала;
А при падении ее
Я загадал желанье этим летом:
Любить, быть пламенным огнем,
Любовью этой быть согретым.
Я лишь хочу, чтоб на закате
Дождем излило мне судьбу;
И я сказал бы: "С меня хватит!
Стань моим Богом наяву!!!"

> *(Turns back to the audience. Continuing from his story about the shopgirl with another story about a different girl)*

but that's
not the reason
they don't let me out
my parents explain it like this:
so they let me out
on the street – when i started going
to the group, i was
not in very good shape – three
or four years ago.
i met a new volunteer
this one was **Olga** (i forgot her last name)
it was nice talking to her
and i asked her to
take me outside in the yard
and there ... the asphalt
and it got windy
So there was pavement with a
curb at the edge

and for some reason I thought
i'll step down
and because of the ledge
i just
fell right over
and my face – i broke a tooth
on the pavement
she stepped away – she was
doing something with the kids,
up ahead
and so i come up with this
gorgeous mess with blood, without
teeth, and she
was losing it –
so that, that – after that
that tooth – mama knew someone
who fixed it –
and then another time inside
the school – on a pipe, i tripped on
the linoleum
and broke it up to the nerve
so ... there it is.
(putting his hands up, an exaggerated shrug)
after that, i started to stay at home
and i told them so many times
but they –
(imitating a scolding, anguished mother's voice)
you fall – your teeth! your head!
and we'll be sitting
by your hospital bed again
like after the accident
(pauses, remembering parents' distress over his near-death)
you can only go places in cars,
if you've called ahead
so that's what the fourteenth was –
i'm only allowed out for things like that
(Spins in his chair toward the window, and looks out for a time. Then
turns, completing a near full rotation, to face the audience. He sighs.

He stands up and crosses to the stationary bike. Slowly, he gets on the
bike but does not begin pedaling. He begins to speak again)

in general i don't sleep very much
i don't set an alarm,
i just say to myself – get up
early
when my brother is getting ready for school
I hear him
then
i get up, i go out to the kitchen
i have some tea – i can't
eat cereal – my stomach
just needs to drink tea. around
seven mama gets ready
and when she leaves, i
take myself back
to my room – and turn on the computer –
VK[2] – and the day begins
i talk to people
i'm chatting – recently especially –
messages are coming in – and i listen
to music, and play games – do you
know the game "heaven"?
i've played it lots of times – they have this
contest. i entered –
there in the game – they made a contest –
"miss heaven" – the sweetest girl.
it was even on the radio
i entered a question on the site and the announcer read it
it was my question about poems.
and she answered – while i was listening.
and i found her page
on VK, and I showed her my poems
and she

---

2 VK is short for VKontakte, a Russian social network that is based on the Facebook
   format and very widely used (more popular than Facebook in this region).

wrote back
she said, that
she liked the poem
she said, "there's something of love in poems"
sometimes i get tired and rest for
awhile
like ten minutes or so i don't do anything
lying down
and eyes closed – really
it's to get a break from the computer –
i forget about time and sometimes
i forget about food
in here
I can do whatever
I want

(He begins pedaling the bike, slowly at first, and then faster and faster)

Portrait III

ALINA

Alina is sitting in a manual wheelchair in a living room decorated in the So-
viet style: a sleeper sofa with cushions covered with a cheap blanket lines one
wall; a red woven rug hangs on the wall above; the opposite wall is lined with
standard-issue seven-foot bookshelf-cabinet units. She is wearing a red sweater
and stretch pants. She is thirty-four, very thin, with dramatic cheekbones. Her
dark heavy hair is pulled back into a low ponytail, and she wears no makeup
or jewelry. Her elbows and wrists rest on the armrests of her wheelchair. When
she moves her arms as she talks, it is clear that her hands and wrists are stiff, her
fingers held steady in a slightly curved position. When she talks, she entertains
herself, sometimes smiling broadly at her own jokes, one side of her smile slightly
wider than the other.

ALINA: Oh good. Come on in here.

        (ALINA waves toward a smaller space set off from the living room area,
        set with a large desktop on a computer desk, and a bookshelf with
        used notebooks, plastic flowers, and some old family photos)

        Mama took the neighbor's daughter home. She's always
        leaving her here on the weekends. She's always, "Aunty
        Alina, Aunty Alina!! *Tyotyenka [TYO-tien-kah]*, let me
        do the computer game!" Children like me.

        This is my room. Well, I don't sleep in here, but I come in
        this room when I want to be alone. I want to show you
        something on the computer.

All my life I've loved information about actors and singers. And not in the sense of who married who, but who was in what movie, and what kind of roles. It used to be hard to find that kind of information. But now –

(imitating a tabloid headline)

"**Mashkov**[3] bought three houses" – the gossip is everywhere. But three houses, they've got to be kidding – it's too many!!

When I'm sitting at home alone, then I like to find brainteaser games and answer the questions. Like right now I'm on VK, and I've got a few games going. My brain may as well get a workout now and then. But in general, I really like to talk to people.

But unfortunately, with most of my friends – talking online can be hard to pull off, it's like pulling teeth. So it gets to the point that I'm fed up with always sending invitations so that people would come visit me. Young people – they can do it. But for us, the generation already in our thirties ... talking on the internet isn't *really* talking to someone.

So anyway, I wanted to tell you about this one comedian on the show Comedy Battle. I usually watch Comedy Battle in the living room. On TV. But sometimes I sit in my room and watch online.

There's a link for all the different channels. So I can find whatever video I want.

(scrolling through videos, looking for the one that she wants)

I have them all memorized – I can tell them apart by the clothes the comedians are wearing. So then if – like – when there's someone else in the room I'll sit and watch it on the computer.

And so during the week when it's boring ... when there's time. And when I'm really looking for a good mood, I'll turn it on.

---

3 Vladimir Mashkov is a well-known actor and director in Russian film and theater whose career spans the Soviet and post-Soviet period, and includes appearances in major Hollywood films.

(ALINA starts scrolling again through a page on the website to look for a video she wants to share, but then thinks of another thing, or, as if responding to a question from an audience member, "what was it like growing up as a kid with a disability here?")

Well, I used to go and spend time at this one center for kids with disabilities – a nonprofit.[4] I mean, since I was little, I've been going once a week, just to hang out with the other kids with disabilities. In those days we pretty much didn't know what we were doing, we would just get together. Then after I grew up, I was working there, as a volunteer, to help with the kids.

We did as much as we could do ourselves, it was all new for us, novel, the methods that we were using, well, through trial and error, on our own.

The point was just to get a change of scenery, and the really important thing ... was that we didn't have enough socializing. We drew pictures, hung out, we tried to put together holiday celebrations, New Years, birthdays. Basically, with almost no money and just our own *sily [SEEL-hee]* – our own strength – we tried to, well, we were trying to figure it out on our own. We got some money from Finnish sponsors – but not very much.

(ALINA's mother – MAMA – enters the other room. She is wearing a house dress, cotton tights, wool socks, and a pair of slippers. She has a small book in her hand, and begins fussing around the room as if looking for the right place to put it away)

Our biggest problem is transportation. A lot of the money was spent on gas. It's expensive. I don't know how it is there now. I haven't been for a long time already ... now the group is sort of homeless. The city took back the space we were using.

---

4 The characters in the play are loosely acquainted by virtue of having grown up or lived for a time with a disability in the same small city. They know one another, but are not necessarily friends. Some of these connections came about in part through foreign-funded nonprofit civil society programs that served families of children with disabilities during the 1990s. Subsequently, by the 2010s, these groups were supplanted with new federally funded municipal psychosocial rehabilitation programming for people with disabilities. Those who became disabled later in life (Vera, Rudak, Anya) may know one another through other social networks.

(MAMA sits down on the sofa in the other room and picks up and begins reading a TV guide printed on cheap newspaper. She eavesdrops on ALINA as she reads)

We got a lot of cast-offs and hand-me-downs – little things that no one liked, and we had mountains of things donated from lots of people.

People know what they need in hospitals and wherever else. But the people who wanted to help us had no concept of what we needed. When we were hungry in the nineties, the whole world helped us.[5] Finland helped us, there was nothing to buy, and through the Lenin Children's Fund, named for **Vladimir Ilich Lenin**, maybe you heard of him, the first ... the first – well, you could say "president" – the first Soviet president.

(then, with winking sarcasm)

Maybe you've heard of him ...

(waits for audience to confirm or deny, then, switching to a well-rehearsed diatribe about contemporary Russian politics)

It's just a lot of people these days are forgetting. A lot of Russians even don't know who Lenin was. Truly, that's how things are here.[6]

MAMA: *(calling from the other room, having overheard; speaking accusingly about the audience)*

---

5 Here, Alina is referring to the years of post-Soviet crisis, when the transition to a market economy led to immense shortages of consumer goods, and the value of money was subject to drastic inflation, effectively leaving many Russians extremely poor, both financially and in terms of the lack of access to basic household necessities. Yet, she gripes, foreign aid for people with disabilities often seemed incongruent with the actual austerity of these real needs, and, while disabilities are sometimes medical conditions, the needs of families with disabled children are not the same as the needs of hospitals and other institutions.

6 Lenin was the first leader of the Soviet Union, a revolutionary communist whose idealistic legacy was followed by the brutal years of Stalinist oppression. By the time Alina's generation grew up, the Soviet Union, which seemed eternal to their parents and grandparents, was suddenly no more. Instead, Alina and her peers grew up in the 1990s and 2000s with large gaps in education about the history of their country as curricula changed and the culture shifted toward the West. In this sense, Alina's statement that her peers "don't know who Lenin is" is at once hyperbolic and polemical, and plausibly true.

They don't know who Lenin is. They don't know!

(then, to the audience)

So who was he? Who is your grandmother! Go and read
about it!

(MAMA begins rummaging in one of the cupboards)

ALINA: The thing is that – everything that happened before us –
we don't remember. It's too bad. We forget – how the
generations that came before us sacrificed. Probably
everywhere it's like that. But I don't know, I'm not sure.
But we *really* have this tendency in Russia. Even, like,
the skinheads here now, the gangs, that are out there.
It means that, that they've totally lost sight of what
previous generations were struggling for.

MAMA: *(Coming into the room with ALINA, but addressing the audience.
She has something in her hand that she's unearthed in the
cupboard.)*

Do you want to see my **Komsomol** ticket?

*(MAMA holds out her Komsomol ticket – a Soviet-era communist youth
ID card. Then, pointing to the ID photo)*

Take a look at this, how I looked.

*(she shows ALINA, who has presumably seen it before, the photo, and
they both laugh)*

ALINA: *(also to audience)*

So skinny, right?!

MAMA: Forty-five rubles a month. That was the wage. The 1960s.
We got forty-five rubles a month, and we lived.

*(MAMA stands for a moment, lost in thought. ALINA looks at her,
waiting to see if she'll speak. After a beat or two, ALINA rolls her eyes
and turns back to the computer. MAMA goes back to the other room,
and begins rustling around in a cupboard, putting the Komsomol card
back in a shoebox in a cabinet)*

ALINA: *(continuing her previous thought)*

So over there in the US, you have your barrier-free
environment, your inclusive education, your models for

special education with young disabled children. Our professionals, our parents – they took all of it from the West.[7] I should know, I got a degree in Special Education. Because of volunteering at the organization, with the kids, I guess. But no one will hire me. Not for pay. Why should I work for free just because I'm disabled? No one will hire one of their own.

I heard that in the West people would go out and protest.

I've been watching Obama. You have elections soon.

The citizen's role, over there you agitate for the future of the country. Here – forget it. Here they might say, Putin was elected, if not Putin, then who?! What's the difference?! We'll still be sitting there in two years thinking, "Why did Putin win? Why didn't someone else?" The thing is, we don't have any reason to protest, and no matter what we do, it will all end up the same ... no matter what.

MAMA: *(from the other room, calling over her shoulder)*
"It will all end up the same" – that's a dangerous way to think, a thoughtless person's – [8]

ALINA: *(rephrasing her own point)*
They'll *tell* us the same thing, no matter what.
I'm not talking about Putin. I'm talking about protesting about *rights*, like for people with mobility impairments.

MAMA: *(coming to the door again, now with another piece of personal memorabilia in hand)*
But – look at it this way: where would we stand, who would we protest to?

---

7 With this comment, Alina suggests that the US is a global leader when it comes to issues of disability access, that disability access is excellent in the US, and that Russia is "worse off" on this front. This idea – that disability access is better in the US than in Russia – is a broad generalization that is commonly held by both Russians and many North Americans. However, as disability studies scholarship – and the lived experience of many people – shows, disability access and social inclusion is an ongoing process, and North Americans with disabilities experience many barriers, and both Russians and Americans with disabilities navigate these barriers to lead exciting lives.

8 The translation here is not precise. The Russian is as follows:
ALINA: То есть, нам нет смысла сидеть, нам по-любому десять раз ...
MAMA: По-любому, этот совсем все развалит, неумный человек.

ALINA: In order to ...

          (trails off, mutters something unintelligible)

MAMA: There's no one.

          (a beat, and then quickly, interrupting and speaking over one another)

ALINA: But why take a stand against Putin? In principle, Putin took charge of every – /thing, how would he not st – /

MAMA: /The ones who – /when Yeltsin left[9] – who didn't take charge of the country, when we lived without pensions, without salar – /

ALINA: And back then when he took office he seemed really wise, that he was passing on power to younger people. I'll say this: for us, Putin is more ... he's the first younger president in the history of Russia. He took office when ... he was only forty.

MAMA: *Medvedev* was even younger.

ALINA: And at his age, Medvedev, he started in 1999. At that point he was what, forty-five or something like that.

MAMA: Everyone else we've had has been fifty, sixty, seventy ...

ALINA: Fifty, sixty already ...

MAMA: And we had *Brezhnev*, who couldn't do anything at all.

ALINA: After him ... /

MAMA: After him they already/

ALINA: ... they got back on course.

MAMA: He couldn't even talk. They just carried him around. And that's it. But they wouldn't even give the time of day to *Gorbachev*, they had a revolution.

---

9 In this exchange, Mama and Alina relate popular opinions about major leaders of Russia since the mid-twentieth century. Yeltsin was the leader of Russia during the initial transition from the Soviet Union, a time of crisis, when Soviet state enterprises – from factories to social services – ceased to function, and many people were thrust into extreme poverty. For a timeline of leaders, see Appendix 3.

ALINA: Gorbachev was an old man too. But all of America was
           backing him, if you can remember? He gave a speech, or
           a lecture, in Washington, I think.

MAMA: And he still gives lectures from time to time.

ALINA: Now he's already eighty-something. Now. And they
           still don't recognize his contributions! Even now they
           criticize him, but criticizing is our favorite thing to do,
           us Russians. I don't know how it is for you Americans,
           but we really love doing nothing, making no effort
           to understand what's happening, but being critical.
           This is what we like to do. That's how we are, it's our
           national character. If a day goes by that we don't criticize
           something, then the day went by in vain.

           *(MAMA nods, then turns back to the other room. She goes in, sits down
           and turns on the TV)*

           Anyway, I've been trying to show you this – this whole
           time – this one person, from the current season of
           Comedy Battle, the TV show. They're updating the cast.
           And there is one guy from *Ufa* [*oo-FAH*, a city in the
           Ural Mountains], he's thirty-one. And they diagnosed
           him with cerebral palsy when he was two years old. The
           same diagnosis as me. He's the first one [disabled person]
           in Russia, I think, to be in the Comedy League. Do you
           know about the Comedy League?

MAMA: *(shouting, her eyes still on her own TV program)*
           It's a comedy competition. And there are teams.

ALINA: They're amateur performers – /

MAMA: *(interrupting)*
           Amateur performers, with their own teams.

ALINA: So, it's humor, jokes.

MAMA: *(still calling from the other room)*
           A certain kind of humor, and jokes. University students
           write the sketches, then they all come out and the teams
           compete.

ALINA: And so, he writes for the team, and he has cerebral palsy. So he participated in this program and they selected him, can you imagine? A person with cerebral palsy. He talks much better than Vakas, but his speech is labored. But the MC on the show, *Pavel Volia*, said to him: "Your act is awesome. You're the man!"... This guy with cerebral palsy.[10]

Sure there are other comedians with cerebral palsy, abroad, in the US.[11] There, people, well, maybe, they're more accepting. But for us, it's totally new. Like, when I saw him for the first time, I was like "Ohhh, wow. Mom, look! And to think that Vakas is shy about reading his poems!"

But here is a person who writes and is also presenting it himself.

Maybe it's hard for us, I don't know, I've always been around other people at home, but not for school.

When I went to high school, they kept me at home. It's called "at-home education." The teachers came twice a week to check my lessons.

I didn't have presentations for the class, it's true. And now I do speak quietly in front of other people. I was taught it's not polite to shout, it's not proper for a formal setting.

MAMA: *(shouting from the other room)*

There's no socializing! That and also, the limited space, the limited people. At home education! Ideas, experiences, the kinds of people you get to know – you're stuck!!

(MAMA, standing, and coming to the door frame, to look in at ALINA)

And then before that – when you were little – a lot of the parents didn't work, but I worked.

(then, to audience)

So I would lock her in the apartment and walk to work, clean the floors as a janitor for three hours ... After a

---

10 The comedian she is describing, Sergeich Kutergin, can be found on his YouTube channel (https://www.youtube.com/user/Yogriss). The videos could be incorporated into the production.

11 For example, Josh Blue, who won a similar televised comedy show in the US (NBC's *Last Comic Standing*) in 2005–6, also has cerebral palsy.

year and a half, I was going into the city to work at the
medical clinic. I would leave keys with the neighbors,
and they would feed her, change her, and sometimes they
brought her over to their place – that was when we were
renting an apartment in a house. But when we moved
here, to a bigger apartment building, I would lock her
in ... they didn't give me medical leave, even when she
was in a cast after an operation ... I walked to work and
locked her in ...

ALINA: You didn't say it right, I was never alone, I always had a lot
of people around ... there were always people around me.

MAMA: I would leave the keys and the neighbors would come, it
was simpler then.

ALINA: I would play with the kids and no one picked on me. It
was only when they grew up a little that they realized
that I couldn't get around ... Even now, everyone in the
building can't believe that I go places, that I do things.

*(MAMA grunts, and nods, and goes back to her spot on the couch and
her program)*

(beat)

Being at home – it makes you think: how did people live
before there was radio, television, telephones? It's like
they didn't live at all ...

Back then if you wanted to see someone you arranged it in
advance, then you just showed up. Wrote it all down in
black and white.

MAMA: Or just went to visit – no warning.

ALINA: Maybe it was better when it was unexpected ... It just falls
on you, like snow on your head – it would be a surprise.

It was just that back then people wanted to communicate in
person more.

(scrolling through the videos again)

This is the one.

(clicks on one video, and hovers the mouse, about to press play)

So – this comedian. He's – he's the first person on Russian
    television who's ... *atypical*. Or – he said in his sketch –
    he's "a person with special effects." There really hasn't
    been anything like this on before.

*(ALINA presses play and one of Sergeich's videos plays, a Russian
comedian performing on stage.[12] The screen might be projected
so that it is also visible to the audience. She stops the video after a
particular joke. ALINA pauses, then addresses the audience.)*

So what's it like, living together, mother and daughter?

We're happy. We live on humor, we start from humor in the
    morning, and everything is all right.

But how else would you live? Like so many others in our
    country. Because most people don't believe what Putin
    says, but comedians, the things that comedians are
    saying, you have to believe in that.

*(thinks for a moment, then as if the audience will know what she's
talking about)*

You know, "we are all like transformers." The movie ...
Comedy Club. It was this one joke ...

*(ALINA reaches for a hairbrush on a nearby shelf, next to a hand mirror
and a cup of pens; holding it like a microphone, she performs the joke
like a comedian presenting a stand-up monologue)*

"I watched that movie *Transformers* – But I didn't get it. So
    what – they can change shapes? That didn't impress me.
    People are better. People are changing all the time. At
    home they're one way, at work, totally different, in the
    elevator completely different, and then on a date, another
    way ..."

So. That's our life ...

Maybe they should have given that joke to **Sergeich.**
    Oporniki ... we're the real transformers. One minute
    you're the volunteer at the charity organization and all
    the kids are tugging on your arm. Then I'm at home and
    I'm the last-minute babysitter for the neighbor's kids.

---

12 Please visit the companion website (www.iwasneveralone.org) to the play for
    video clip examples.

Then I'm chatting online, just another friend typing,
"When are you coming over to hang out with me – are
you free next weekend?" Or I'm clicking the video links
– one more like for that video – just another mouse click.
Or I'm getting carried downstairs just to sit outside and
read my book for a while. Transformers ...
I know all the scripts. I can play any of the parts.

Portrait IV

SERGEI

Sergei enters, walking slowly, with an uneven gait; his ankles turn steeply out-ward at an angle where they join his feet. He greets the audience, as if to a host upon entering an acquaintance's apartment. He is carrying a small plastic bag and wearing a winter coat, khaki pants, a scarf, hat, and boots. He sits on a stool and changes his boots for a pair of slippers. He takes off his hat and scarf and puts them in the pocket of his winter coat. He has neatly cut brown hair, short sideburns, and is clean-shaven. He walks slowly across a space to an area where there is a small kitchen table. There is an electric kettle on a counter, and the table is set with two teacups, saucers, a sugar bowl, and a small teapot with loose leaf tea. He sets a packet of wafer cookies on the table, and takes off his winter coat, hanging it somewhere nearby. He is wearing a cotton sweater over a polo shirt. The tea kettle has just begun to audibly boil. Sergei speaks thoughtfully, earnestly, with a sincere gentleness. He has the habit of pausing to think back over what he's said, and then, agreeing with himself, saying "Da" (the Russian word for "yes," in this context, "right" or "yeah") and then going on or trailing off, mulling over his next sentence with a long "So ..." (in Russian, "vot"). He's a go-with-the-flow kind of guy.

Sergei moves to the table and takes a seat on a backless, chair-height stool.

SERGEI: I like when we meet at your place for interviews! I brought wafer cookies this time. Always show up with something sweet – that's what my mom told me!

(He opens a packet of wafer cookies and pours some into a small waiting plate on the table. SERGEI's cell phone rings, and he takes it out of his pocket. It's an old flip phone, not a smartphone)

It's my mom. She probably doesn't know where I went.

(Answers the phone. Then, in Russian or English:)

Da, Mama ... at the interview ... in a taxi ... of course I remembered the cookies ... Okay. Bye.

[*Da, mama ... Na intervu ... V taksi ... konechno sladkie ne zabyl ... Okei. Paka.*] [*Dah, maH-ma ... naw een-TARE-view ... Ff-tax-ee ... cone-YESH-no slawd-KEY-yeh nyeh za-BWHEEL*]

(Then, SERGEI thinks, and then looks up to the audience)

Have some cookies!

(He offers some of the wafer cookies to the audience, as if to a friend sharing the tea and cookies)

So what questions do you have for me this time? Did you like the last interview?

(Looks at the audience as if for a response. Then, as if answering a question from the audience)

The *internat*?[13]

So this kindergarten – this kindergarten had just opened, a special education one. So. I – I went there. The first class.

I, you know, I feel like it's a big thing – my whole life, we've been doing experiments on me – I am always surviving experiments!

(with gentle irony, describing well-intentioned incompetence)

Perezhivau eksperimenty! [*pear-reh-ZHEE-vai-you ehk-spair-ree-MYEHN-tee*].

And when the special kindergarten had a graduating class, it graduated the children to the special school. So. To the *internat*. And so, the question never came up: whether

---

13 *Internat* is a Russian word that can be translated as "boarding school"; however, in the context of disability, the word is sometimes closer to "institution," given that for many people with disabilities of Sergei's generation across the former Soviet Union, the segregated education of the *internat* was the only option – inclusive and integrated education for children with disabilities was not available in the

I would study at some regular school. They had already designated that I would go to the *internat*. And ... I went on to study there.

(pause, thinking)

So, our class wasn't very big. In my class there were seven people.

So ... each person had something different. *Da* – some had serious problems, some had moderate, and then just a little. And some for whom it was practically invisible. So – there are different degrees of impairment. ***Zabolevaniye [zah-bowl-leh-VAWN-knee-yeh]***. So, and of course in life it works out so that it's easier for those whose impairments are less visible.

Mine is moderate. I think. So, I have a mid-level, sort of.

What was it like? It was a full life. We celebrated holidays together, concerts ... and we had theatrical performances – I did plays, from the seventh or eighth grade on. They discovered me when I recited a poem in the seventh or eighth grade. *The Letter to Eugene **Onegin**,*[14] I think, something like that. And – they noticed and invited me to join, it was sort of like, the theater club. And – I have all of it on video.

(smiling)

If you want to watch it ...

(His phone rings again. He looks at the screen, his suspicions are confirmed, and he silences the call)

Mama is calling again.

Soviet Union. Sergei's generation, growing up in the 1990s, were the first in his city to be offered integrated education. On the other hand, education at an *internat* is indeed specialized, and many *internats* are and were staffed by highly trained, dedicated experts; efforts to improve special education in mainstream schools came about thanks to parent advocacy in Sergei's city in the second decade of the twenty-first century.

14 *The Letter to Eugene Onegin* is a famous novel in verse, by Pushkin, adapted as an opera and in various other performative genres. A Russian speaker referencing this is like citing a well-known work of Shakespeare. Sergei here is likely imprecise in recalling the piece, as the novel itself is titled *Eugene Onegin*, while the letter refers to a specific scene in which a female character composes a love letter to Onegin (in the following scene, Onegin himself responds in person).

How has it changed? Now there's a trend that those kids
who *can* care for themselves independently – all of
a sudden, they are going to the regular city schools,
according to their school district. So, that's how it's
working out, you know? If before, there was a tendency,
if you had disability, then you go to the *internat*, like
everyone else with disability.

Because before, the thinking was that it would be difficult
for these people to adapt to a general school environment
because they are not *like* everyone else. So that's what
they thought before. And so they sent everyone right to
the *internat*, so that there wouldn't be any questions or
problems.

But now – it's come around to a situation where, if you
communicate well, regardless of whether or not you have
difficulty getting around, the important thing is that you
can hold a conversation and get on with people. Then, in
that case, *you* can go to a regular school.

And so the *internat*, then is left for those kids who,
due to their condition can't communicate, and don't
understand, like, if you try asking them a question. These
kids are the ones that have to go to the *internat* now. Of
course – everything's different. Everything's

(looking down at his hands)

totally changed. And – well, it's not *embarrassing*, but it's
weird somehow.

(the phone rings again, and he silences it again, very quickly)

Some people think that it's good when a person with special
needs – um – well,

(trying out the politically correct term "with disability")

with disability, yeah with disability, when they send
him to the mainstream school. And then he more or less
adapts. It might be hard for him, or, maybe – well, he has
to adapt somehow. And then there are those people who
really take that perspective.

(small pause)

But then some parents really are of the opinion that – what
for? Because they think that, here in Russia, with our
government, um ... people have hardly seen people with
disabilities, right? In our time it was even embarrassing
to talk about it. *Stidno.* [*STEED-no.* Embarrassing.] Um,
they more or less didn't talk about it. So, for that reason,
well, parents have different opinions. Some think that
really, it's unnecessary, that's true. Maybe that's shocking
because it seems to you

(meaning Americans, addressing the audience)

that it's not right, where you're from they accept
everyone at the mainstream school. And so, there are
those who expect that a certain kind of person will be
assigned to the *internat*.

And now, after high school, in 2007, right, in college they
also organized

(with sarcasm)

an "experimental" group – of people with disabilities – at
Petrozavodsk Teacher's College. And I ended up there,
again, as part of the very first group, and it turned out
that once again, it was an experimental situation: *What
happens if people with disabilities get higher education?*

(pause)

Da.

They renovated a classroom for us, a philanthropic
something-or-other, from Germany, I think. And so we
went there, along with the other students.

Mama said – Go! Go! Participate, see how they are! She
meant, talk with the other people. To try to talk to them.
But, of course, I didn't really talk to them. *Da.* Well, it
didn't really work out.

I hadn't had that experience, of going to the mainstream
school, of getting tossed into the crowd ... The only sense
of that that I had was in college. We had our group, and –
I went to class with a group that – besides me, there were,
I think three people with disabilities, and all the rest – we
had thirty people – all the rest were normal.

So ... I wouldn't say that we had a *friendly* relationship. With these people, the normal students. But you could say that we were *neutral* in our attitudes toward one another. That is, people weren't cruel, there wasn't a sense of cruelty, there wasn't really anything, and it also wasn't friendly. It was just like – *sharing space*.

And we still meet up, even after finishing college. We meet up every now and then, like three times a year. *Da.*

(as he talks, SERGEI is formulating his opinion – he has never been asked to offer this perspective before, and he's just coming to his position as he explains it)

But, well, you see how it ends up for us – I mean, talking about the integration of people with disabilities into society. And we just – a person with a disability – so say they take him in the mainstream school, right? And at that point, maybe they're not even thinking about the fact that it might be really hard for him there. Um, because *here in Russia*, we, in the first place – well, we don't hate people with disabilities, they don't *hate* them, but they are somehow hidden away from society. So, because of that, it will only be with difficulty that they accept him at the ... mainstream school. For the person himself, the one with a disability, I think. There will be difficulties.

And even – people from college – even, for example, online, on VKontakte, it's funny, right, on VKontakte, you add people, and then, after three years, you look, and that one isn't there anymore, that one is gone, that one is gone from your list of friends. So, I don't know. Maybe they – the girls, maybe they got married. *Da.* But even so, when I write a message, if I write a message – I write a big message for everyone, I write to everyone, and only a few of them read it, and maybe it's because of that they deleted me. I don't know. But, maybe it's just like that. Like that they unfriended me. *Nedobovialis'.* [*knee-dough-baw-VAH-lease.* Unfriended.]

(SERGEI's phone rings again, he silences it. Then, as if explaining this latest phone call to the audience)

Mama always thinks that I'm going to bother someone.

(imitating MAMA)

Are you bothering people? Come home now!

(in his own voice again)

No, I'm not bothering anyone.

(pauses, then looks at the audience and grins)

You know, I was talking about movies before. About what kind of movies I like to watch. When I'm home alone? I like to watch war movies lately. There's something else about that. I watch all kinds of films – American, Russian, whatever.

And you know, people say that Americans don't like hard-to-watch films, that in American films, at the end, the main character always ends up winning, with his hands raised, triumphant. Not as a symbol of relief that he got through something, but just the opposite, that he has won because he was always going to win.

Mama says that it's better to watch American films because they have happy endings, they're not as sad. Even if the main character is fighting a thousand enemies, he still wins. She likes to watch

(imitating MAMA again)

something light.

But in ours, there are often these shocking endings. Like, they'll kill the main character in the final frames. It's surprising when they do that. Especially in the very last moments. And everything is supposed to work out well –

(making a joke, switches to heavily accented English)

Kheppi End!

(then, with glee)

Nope!

Portrait V

RUDAK

Rudak is sitting in a wheelchair, at one of several café tables in a small nightclub. A stage is set for a rock concert, with a drum set, mics, and mic stands. Two band-mates are unloading gear in the background, crossing in and out, unraveling mic cords, and so forth. Rudak is wearing a crocheted skull cap, and a collared button-down short-sleeve shirt – the kind that is boxy and alternative, not for a businessman. He is relaxed, leaning back, one arm on the table, jovial and open.

RUDAK: I only have a few minutes, and then we'll have to start our sound check. If we don't do it properly
(raising his voice so that a man in jeans and dress shirt hurriedly carrying a trumpet case to the stage – the TRUMPET PLAYER – can hear)
the horns always drown out my vocals!
(The TRUMPET PLAYER turns and smirks and gestures in mock offense to RUDAK, before heading back out the way he came. RUDAK laughs)
I've been with these guys for years. At first, it was just me and the other guitarist. Then we found our bassist – he's a piece of work – once we had him, there was no going back. We added the horns when we did our second album. Our newest one – *Live Journal* – was our third album. Local releases. We only play shows three, maybe four times a year but we always get a good crowd.

We're all busy. I've got my film projects, the other guys
all work normal jobs, the trumpet player is also in the
city orchestra. So it's enough that we get to get together
and practice now and then. Usually, they come to me, or
some of the guys come pick me up and carry me out to
one of their cars.

Just like everyone else in this godforsaken city, I live in one
of the older buildings without – without ramps, without
elevators. A couple flights of concrete steps between me
and the rest of the world. So if you want to talk about
disability access, I can tell you plenty about inaccess.

*(BASSIST, a man wearing black jeans and a black turtleneck and
carrying two guitar cases, crosses to the stage. He sets the cases on the
stage)*

BASSIST: *Rudak, normal'no?* [Rudak, everything good?]

RUDAK: *Da, drug. Normal'no. Schas budu.* [Yeah, dude. I'm good.
I'll come help in a minute.]

BASSIST: *Da, ladno! Otdikhai, Voloden'ka! My yesho kombik
postavim.* [Don't you worry! Take it easy, *Volodienka*,
m'dear! We still have the amps to load in.]

(BASSIST heads back to where he came from to exit)

RUDAK: *(again to audience)*
He's giving me a hard time.
(giggles)
I never do any of the setup work or unload, I'm the special
flower. The pampered front man.
(smiles to himself)
You heard about the case at the train station? The trains
have these new accessible cars. Fully renovated.
European style. State of the art.
But do you think you can get to the platform in a
wheelchair? Forget it. Two long flights of steps. AND –
they have these new tickets. Reduced fares with your
disability status card. But in order to buy one of these
tickets you need to present your card in person to the

agent in the ticket hall. Where do you think they put
the new ticket hall? At the end of the platform, totally
inaccessible from the street, two flights of granite steps.
So as long as you have a wheelchair that can also fly, you'll
have a great experience on Russian trains.

*(BASSIST crosses again, carrying an amp. RUDAK follows him with his
eyes until he sets it down on the stage. BASSIST crosses and exits again)*

So Svetlana and the gang, we got together and we wrote
a letter to Moscow. And then we wrote an official
complaint. And eventually, bum-bum-bum-bum,
seven months, a year later, we finally get a response.
From whatever official office in the city government.
"The Train Station will be made Fully Accessible for
the Disabled in the course of the Next Scheduled
Renovation."

That was a year ago. So what do you think has happened
since then? Nothing! The reconstruction is scheduled
to take place two years from now. Therefore, until that
time, everything is frozen. But – *actually* – nothing
will happen – I wouldn't even be surprised if nothing
happens in two years!!

But at least at the train station there are porters hanging
around, and people carrying suitcases. And they'll
carry you up if you ask. What's worse is all of these
storefronts. Do you think the snotty twenty-two-year-old
at the shoe store is going to come out and carry you up
the steps? Forget it. Half the places have no accessibility
elements at all – just steps. And then the other half
are building these totally useless ramps that have no
relationship to reality.

Why – why are they cropping up, eh? Because – First of
all. The people who are building these ramps, they are
doing it so that – so that the ramp *exists*. So if someone
asks them, "Do you have a ramp?" – like, if someone
asks, not a person with a disability, but a person – let's
say, from some kind of committee, or something like
that. Someone or other comes with a clipboard and

whatever documents, they'll put a *check mark*. That's it –
access for the disabled is accounted for.

I don't know about other countries, but in Russia, when it
comes to building ramps and entranceways, they don't
ask *us* to be consultants – no one who is a representative
of organizations that work with people with mobility
impairments, or people who are wheelchair-users
themselves. They – create ramps that *seem like*, to them,
what a ramp should be. They forget to install handrails,
or they make a really steep incline, like, or the ramp is
just leaning up against a wall even.

*(TRUMPET PLAYER crosses carrying a bunch of coiled cables. He
distributes various coils to separate parts of the stage. RUDAK
continues talking without paying attention to the trumpet player's
actions)*

This way of doing things, it's every man for himself. And –
these people think that – it'll never happen to them.
That, so, *you're* sitting in a wheelchair, that's obvious, it's
how it's somehow *supposed* to be. But it's not something
that could happen *to me*. *MNE?! [min-YEH?!]*[15]

(With the word mne, *RUDAK gestures emphatically toward the center
of his own chest, perhaps pounding it to punctuate an expression of
injustice. He goes on without pause)*

Never. Not to him, or to any of his family members. [So I
bring it up, and] people wave their hands and say, well
nothing is equipped around here. Take a look around –
there's nothing comfortable about living in a block
of Soviet concrete in the frozen north – who cares if
you're in a wheelchair or not! So the same guys who are

---

15 *Mne* is the dative case of the personal pronoun. This form of the pronoun means
literally "to me." It is more typical in Russian than in English, which has the habit
of always speaking about the self as the subject or actor of a sentence. Here, as in
many Russophone constructions, Rudak is describing how an unjust social system
acted *on* him. The gesture that is associated with the dative case in Russian is always action *toward* the self, located in the center of the breastbone. An actor might
gesture outwards with the word "never," but speaking the word "mne" in Russian
is never accompanied by a gesture away from the center of the body, and to see an
actor do so will produce an odd dissonance for Russian speakers in the audience.

doing all of this – building these useless ramps – they're suffering too. So, if there's a way to do it cheaply, to save a little money, then it seems to them that no one's ever going to show up and demand a working ramp.

(The BASSIST and TRUMPET PLAYER cross, each with another amp, and begin setting them around the stage, plugging cables. They confer for a second, then look to RUDAK.)

BASSIST: *Hey Rudak! What's the story with the set list??*

RUDAK: *(in mock anger)*

Whaddya askin' me now, pal, can't you see I'm doing an interview?!

(chuckles, then, softening)

We put the paper in the guitar case.

(RUDAK turns back to audience. BASSIST and TRUMPET PLAYER nudge some equipment here and there, and then exit)

So it's really like that! Like – so I know someone in Moscow. He has a car. According to the law, he's entitled to an individual parking space. So – the parking space is painted yellow with the handicap symbol in the middle – but no one pays any attention. The parking space is always taken. People just park there. So – this guy, he went to, well, to the director of – whatever state office where they deal with these kinds of issues. And he says to the agent – "I'm still stuck: the painted symbol doesn't work. There needs to be some kind of barrier so that only I can park there." And what did the agent say to him? "Well, what would we do if all the disabled people came and said the same thing?" So that's the logic! "We could do this for you, quietly, so that no one knew about it. But then what if ten more disabled drivers come in? And we have to build separate parking spaces for all of them?" So he argued, "But by law, isn't it required?" And he proved that he had a right to this, and so they did build it for him. It's just that he wasted about ... about a *year* on this, maybe.

So, now, finally, thank god, he got the authorities to put
this ...

(thinking of the word)

this barricade, or a barrier? With some kind of lock so that
he could be the only one to open it. So ...

So there you have it – *that's* our "barrier-free environment."

Okay, but look. I know that this is a problem in other
countries too, not just in Russia. When I was in Germany,
when we were shooting the documentary project there,
when we pulled up to

the bus station in the paratransit van, someone had taken
the handicap space, just pulled in there, a regular car
with no sticker. So it's not just in Russia. But that's
how people are. Your average guy wants things to be
convenient for himself, not for people with disabilities.
And sometimes – even – he'll hold it against you, "Ugh,
come on." But if we were to trade lives and he had to
live life in a wheelchair, well, then he'd see what's good
about accessibility ...

But no one wants to trade places. But, they also don't want
to do anything to make life easier for the guy in the
wheelchair. No one cares about this problem ... except
for the few of us who have to deal with it.

Unless they're helping, pitying us poor helpless cripples.

(disparagingly)

Russia.

(then, patriotically)

Rossiya!!

I can get sort of romantic about it though. *Our Motherland.*
Have you heard our song? The one about Japan? It goes
like this.

*(Begins to hum, then sing. TRUMPET PLAYER and BASSIST finish up
what they're doing, and turn to watch, hands on hips, slowing down
after the period of activity. Then, RUDAK pausing in the midst of his
hum)*

We'll play it. Later on.

(resuming the song)

... I said to her ...
run away with me
*In **Petrozavodsk** I have*
a two-room apartment ...
We'll play it.

(fade out as a recording of the song, by the band Orkester Kto Kak Mozhet, picks up where his vocals began)

Portrait VI

ANYA

Anya's apartment is newly renovated, with textured wallpaper, and a new refrigerator with a small collection of magnets. There is a kitchen table, with a large bowl with clementines and some clear plastic bags of tea biscuits and cookies – the kind you buy by the pound – in it. Anya comes in, directing her electric wheelchair with a small joystick. She has neatly styled bobbed hair with bangs and is wearing lightly applied feminine makeup. Her jewelry is gold, including delicate earrings and a necklace with a small diamond and sapphire pendant. Her blouse is clean and new-looking, her pants are loose and have an elastic waist, and on her feet she wears slip-on flats. She has an unembellished flip phone on a tether around her neck. The back of her wheelchair includes a very high headrest, and she leans her head against it, as if saving the muscle strength in her neck for later. When she moves her arms, she does so minimally, conserving energy, using facial expressions rather than hand gestures to punctuate her speech. Her speech starts out polished and professional, but also snarky, and with a sharp sense of irony: she is talking to someone that she considers a peer. She laughs with her eyes, her mouth closed, a light chuckle.

Anya turns in her chair to face the audience, as if greeting a guest who has just come in.

ANYA: So how do you like my new apartment?
          It feels like it's been a long time coming.
          (driving in a small circle and gesturing to a living room area)

This is the common room. There's no furniture yet, but
I'm getting a sofa, probably, and then, I'll also put, like,
a bunch of folding chairs and something like an easel
with paper or a whiteboard in here. So I'll be able to host
group work sessions and individual therapy here.

(raising her eyebrows and adding ironic emphasis)

I've got a home office – can you believe it?

(ANYA goes into the kitchen area, and parks herself near the table)

So, like I said, I've been trying for ages to figure out how
to do private practice on the side. And now I can finally
quit my second job – it was too far to drive, anyway,
to the rehab center out in the country. Now I'm just
working at the agency in town, and, well, once I get this
going ...

I want to do counseling for everyone – people with
disabilities and also people who are just normal.
And group sessions too. Why should I have separate
groups?

Everyone is struggling with the same problems: self-
actualization, to find some kind of understanding of
yourself, to resolve conflicts and build relationships. So
anyway,

(winkingly)

I guess I'm pushing limits there.

And I want to have a group for parents. I mean parents
of children with disabilities, the parents who are just
coming to terms with things.

There are all these moments – stories that my friends
online – people with my condition, or other ones – tell
me. About things that their parents did to them. Abuse.
Refusing to take them places. Leaving them alone for
days at a time. But this mentality ... it's not all the fault
of the moms. You have to understand ...

A long time ago, years ago, in Soviet times, we had a kind
of ideological movement, when they tried to build a
"healthy society." So they took all the people who were
born with disabilities and they hauled them off and

locked them up somewhere ... so that they were out of sight. So, that's probably where it comes from, more or less ... or else ... I don't want to say anything bad about the church ... But I was just dealing with this problem, that for some reason or other the church calls *the disabled* "the defective strata of the population ..."

(indignantly)

Why *defective?!* ... Basically, if you tell a person over and over again that he's a pig, eventually he'll end up oinking. If the church – this great institution that's been so meaningful for people – goes and says "Yes, you have to help the disabled, they're feeble," then people with disabilities end up thinking, "Well, we need help. So let them come and help us." It creates a wrong-headed understanding of your own existence. So, that's what I'm working against ...

It's because of moments like these that I think that it's really important to work with parents right now so that they can raise their kids with disabilities normally. So many parents are doing things all wrong: you really have to start when they're small ... As soon as a child with a disability is born, there should be some kind of psychological assistance for the parents, so that they don't take the birth of their child as a *tragedy*.

(with assurance)

It's not a tragedy, that this particular kid was born ... For instance, kids with Cerebral Palsy are born ... Yes, they have physical impairments, but they have bright minds. So much of the time, they can move mountains – as long as you teach them that they can.

Self-perception. ***Vospriyatiye [vos-pre-YAH-tee-yeh]*** ... It seems to me that the main thing is self-perception. The relationship to yourself, the relationship to life, to society, to family, the relationship to your own disability ... This is the most important thing. If you can get *this* right from an early age ... From an early age, from diapers, and only grow up that way ...

Just like a snowball gets bigger as it rolls, and if you were
    born with a disability and bit by bit they shield you, pad
    the blows, so that you never feel a bump ... then you
    don't learn anything ... it's the same as with any child ...
    he's born and you teach him.
So I at least had some years of normal upbringing before
    my condition started to surface. And then my mom's
    whole life shifted so that she could care for me.

*(Rock music – a Russian radio station playing Deep Purple or Guns N
Roses – is switched on, or maybe a door opens, the sound drifting in
from another room. ANYA pauses, acknowledging the noise. Then,
explaining the noise)*

That's Larissa. She's here cleaning for me.
But we're talking about the meaning of the word

(pronouncing the Russian word for disabled)

een-val-leed. There's something about the word, *een-val-
    leed.* Right? *Disabled.*
What I mean to say is ... that – take a person who is
    physically healthy but doesn't want to do anything. He
    doesn't work, he doesn't make life better for himself.
    I could say that in a way he is an *invalid.* But by that
    measure ... at the same time, I might not say the same
    about a person with physical impairments ...
Like, take our friend the rock musician. I wouldn't call him
    an *een-val-leed,* because he is very self-actualizing. So
    to call him disabled ... You could call him a person *with
    physical impairments,* to acknowledge that his body isn't
    totally ordinary. But ...
There was one kind of funny moment when I was getting
    my psychology degree. It was when I was writing my
    graduate thesis. My topic was "social-psychological
    adaptation of people with disabilities in the period of
    early and middle adulthood with serious impairments"
    (including my own illness). So, then, because I couldn't
    get enough people for the study, I included another
    class of disability. So, more or less, it was all people with

disabilities. Because I was a contrary student,[16] I did all
the research myself and wrote the paper myself. I had
100 people with disabilities. I had to give out surveys
and get responses from everyone. And I just got so
tired of it, I was sitting there and not being able to
understand

(with emphasis)

who among us is *abnormal.*

(laughs)

And then, one day I am going into the lecture hall – I went
to school with normal students – so I'm rushing into
the lecture hall after one by one surveying my disabled
people and I just let out "Good lord, I've had it with
these disabled people!"

And the girls all looked at me bewildered. I'm disabled
myself and I'm talking about my fellow *invalidi* like that –
So after that, I thought to myself, now I *do* know what a
"normal disabled person" is: it's a disabled person who
can say, "I've had it with all these disabled people!"

(laughs)

Get it? It's just the same as when a normal person can say,
"Agh! These neighbors are getting on my nerves!" It's
the same – like …

*(Trails off. Then, ANYA's phone begins to ring – a typical pre-
programmed ringtone song. ANYA begins shouting to someone in the
other room)*

Lariska! Lah-REE-SKAH!! *Telefon zvonit. Prikhodi,
otkrivai, pozhaliusta!* [*tell-le-FOWN zz-vough-NEET.
Pree-khod-DEE, ought-KREE-VAI, po-ZHAL-oo-sta.*
The phone is ringing! Come open it, please!]

*(LARISSA rushes in, wearing a kerchief and sweats and rubber house
shoes, pulling off rubber gloves. A little disheveled. ANYA nods.*

---

16 Many Russian master's students at that time did not write their own MA papers
but paid someone else to do so.

LARISSA reaches for the phone, which ANYA is now holding in her hand, the lanyard still around her neck. LARISSA flips it open and places it at ANYA's ear. ANYA mouths to LARISSA)

Spasibo. [**Spa-SEE-bah.** Thank you.]

(LARISSA blink-nods in affirmation, and steps back to lean against the kitchen counter. ANYA speaks into the phone)

All-YO? ... Da, sizhu s podruzhkoi ... Da, prikhodi ... Da, obed my uzhe gotovyli ... Davai chai pyom ... Davai ... Davai. Davai. [Hello? ... Yes, I'm sitting here with a friend ...

(nodding to acknowledge the audience as that friend)

Sure, come by ... Yes, we already made lunch ... Let's have tea ... Okay ... Okay, okay.]

(The conversation over, ANYA lets the phone fall to the end of the lanyard. Using her chest as a leverage point, she closes the flip phone to end the call. She sighs, and sits for a minute to recoup after the work of shouting)

LARISSA: *Tak.* [So.]

(looking at ANYA, who has turned her chair so that she can face LARISSA without moving her head)

Pit' budesh'? [I'm going to have something to drink. Do you want something?]

(ANYA nods. LARISSA pours herself some water and drinks. She takes another cup, this one a very light, cheaply made plastic one, and adds barely a half-inch of water to it from the pitcher. Still facing the counter, looking for something, LARISSA asks)

Gde trubochka tvoia? [Where's your straw?]

ANYA: *My s Katei vse perelozhili. Tam gde lezhat vilki.* [Katya and I rearranged things. It's by the forks.]

(LARISSA opens a drawer, and takes out a pink plastic drinking straw with a bend in it, the kind you would buy in a pack for a child's birthday party. She places the straw in the cup and adjusts the bend. She turns and puts the cup in ANYA's hand. ANYA slowly raises the cup to her mouth, puts her lips around the straw, and drinks)

LARISSA: *(briefly)*
            Ye-SHOW? [More?]

ANYA: ***Nyet, spasibo.*** [No, thank you.]
            (LARISSA takes back the cup, rinses it quickly, along with her own, and puts them back in the dish drain. She turns back to ANYA)

LARISSA: ***Nu, cho? Vsyo, ya poshla.*** [Well, so? I'm all finished, so I'm going to get going.]

ANYA: ***Khorosho.*** [Okay.]

LARISSA: ***V chetverk uvidemsia.*** [I'll see you Thursday.]
            (ANYA nods. LARISSA exits, back in the direction she came from)

ANYA: *(ANYA again addresses the audience)*
            Ohhh, moving here is good. Before, in my parents' apartment, I had my own room. But I had the idea to live on my own, like … it was, it was growing. Growing-growing-growing inside of me for a long time. And then it sort of crashed over me like a wave … It just flooded over me in one moment.
            I was sitting in the kitchen in my parents' apartment with this one girl. She had come from *Louhi*, in this tiny village way up North, and she lived with us for a while. But then with my nephews it got to be too much, so she moved out, but we liked each other, and she had come to visit me. And she and I were talking. She is saying that she has to move somewhere, but she doesn't make much money, and it's scary to move, to rent an apartment, and everything. And I, like, I am sitting there and saying to her, "Listen, like, would it be possible for us to live together?" And I sort of inserted my own interests, because I can't live alone, you know? Well, so. And she, like, her eyes lit up – "Let's do it, I'm in." So, I got her out of *Louhi*.
            She lived here while we were doing the renovation, in the middle of the mess. What a disaster. Well, so, so basically I renovated these rooms little by little, starting with the

toilet and bathroom.[17] I was thinking that I wouldn't
have enough money. I had some savings anyway. I had
been saving for a long time. I got the apartment, ponied
up the money. So.

So I started with the bathroom and toilet. Then ... a friend
of mine said to me, "We'll wallpaper your room for
you, we'll just do it ourselves." So I figured, they can
do it, they'll do it, and that's it. My friends are so
great. So they started this whole big mess here. They
were doing it as quickly as possible ... Then she did
the hallway. Then I'm like, "That's enough." So then
she started to do the big room. And I had used up all
my money of course. I was putting everything I was
making at work into this, and I was already coming
to the end of my savings. I was spending it like it was
nothing. So.

But what did I decide to move for? I knew that I had to
organize a workspace around myself, I mean at home,
in a living space. But there, at my parents', with kids, it
didn't work, my nephews were always coming in and
out. And someone was always staying over. Someone
is coming to visit. Or my dad was roaming around. Or
there was some kind of commotion about something,
even when people were coming to see me. Is this, like, is
this what it's going to be like? So, if I were going to see
clients, it would be a disaster.

(checking in with her listener)

I mean, can you imagine?

It's just that – you know – when you live with your
parents – it's one thing. You think: "Geez! Where would
I go?" You know, parents are parents. They meddle in
everything. It has to be that way, they have to know.
About everything, you know, every last thing.

And especially in my ... in my situation, right?

---

17 As in much of Europe, in Russian apartments, the bathroom and toilet are generally two separate but adjacent rooms – one with a sink and bathtub, the other with
a toilet.

(humorously)

And, I mean, shit, without my mom I can't even put my underwear on. Or do the things I want to do, ultimately.

(imitating her mom)

"Why did you put those ones on? Why didn't you put on these ones?"

(imitating her own exasperated response)

"Well, I don't want to wear those!! I wanted these ones."

So ... So that's ... it's good to be here.

Well, and like, the renovation took two months. And it was ... everything was ready somewhere around the end of February and it was ready to go, I could have moved in already. But then I had these long tortured conversations with my dad.

He wouldn't talk to me for two weeks, basically, he didn't talk to me at all. He basically didn't talk to me at all.

Then shit hit the fan. I don't remember what it was about. He just started acting like a jerk, you know? Obviously he has some kind of intense overprotectiveness. I understand that he's afraid for me, he's really afraid. So. And that he's worrying about all of it. And he doesn't understand ... My mom ... My mom more or less is the one who cares for me. It's hard for my mom. My mom said, "I'm tired. Let's hope it goes well. Try it, and we'll see what happens."

I have to try, you understand. I won't live out my days with my parents. They're not immortal. There's no avoiding that. Well, so. And ...

(pause)

I couldn't get past it all with him. With my dad. And so, I kept my mouth shut, and I left. I wrote him a letter. My dad. Because, you know, it had turned into the kind of situation where as soon as I started to say something, he would just start yelling, and I would start to cry.

So in it, I very plainly explained – in this letter – like, *Papa. What did you raise me for and give me an education? So that one day, you could say to me that I am too seriously ill?*

And that I can't do anything for myself? You helped me get
two – two – professional degrees. So what for? So that they
could hang out on the shelf? I want to do something, to change
things somehow. With my own means. And while you are
opposed, while you are opposed to it, you could be helping me
to stand on my own two feet.

(pause)

It's not that I live under your thumb, you know? In your
custody. But that, that you would want to see some growth,
that I can do something myself, I can't, but that I can on my
own. It will be nice for you.

My mom said to him, "What's wrong with you? Sixty-four,
you're sixty-four years old." My mom is sixty-three.
"Well, geez, you aren't young." So, my dad …

(starting a new thought)

I just think about my friend. Her mother died. In two
months, if you can imagine, her mom died. So she was
healthy, healthy and then – BAM! – that's it. No mom.
And the girl was like, she was in my situation, pretty
much the same, you know? She is thirty-five also. And
what happened? She was left with no one. She didn't
have anyone at all … They were in a hurry to find
someone there who would care for her and everything.
Is that how things should be? I don't want that. Or
worse, an institution. I want to already be somehow, in
some way prepared, so that I have some way of being on
my own and everything.

So I say to my dad: "Papa, look, if it doesn't work for me,
then, I'll come back and live with you again. I'll *live*, dad,
you know? Or else I'll say, Papa, okay, it didn't work
out."

Yesterday I went over for my things. There he was, treating
me like a stranger. I'm like, so this is how it's going to
be, like strangers? And I'm planning to go for spring
holidays next weekend.

And … a few days ago I went by with some friends and, it
was a holiday, and when I came in he was sort of drunk.

He was sitting on the couch in his room. I, like, go over
and say, "Papa, while I have five days off, I want to bring
that other couch over." He's like, "Over where?" And
I say, "Papa, to the apartment of course." And I start to
leave. And he's like, my dad is like, "We'll bring you
your fucking couch."
"When will you bring it? Will you bring it tomorrow?"
He's like, "Okay, tomorrow."
My eyes basically fell out of my head, I was so surprised.
"My letter for you is lying there."
And he says to me, "I read it."
And I say, "Good for you, you read it."
He's like, "It's an inappropriate letter."
And I say, "Why? It's a perfectly appropriate letter. Why
is it an inappropriate letter? It's a perfectly appropriate
letter."

*(LARISSA crosses, going from the back of the apartment to the exit.
She's hardly recognizable, now dressed in street clothes, cheap jeans
and a yellow top, and fully made-up, with glossy pink lipstick. When
she's just off-stage she yells back)*

LARISSA: *An'! Don't forget the laundry detergent!!*

ANYA: *Okay! Have a good week!*

LARISSA: *Bye!*

ANYA: *(looking toward the main room)*
So anyway, the couch will go over there.

*(She rolls back into the main room. She turns her chair to face the
audience, as if looking out a large window)*

I really like living on the first floor. I can see everything
from the window.

*(she watches LARISSA, who's put on a coat and boots and a hat, walk
across, as if outside)*

And I have a ramp at the front stoop. They already built it
for me. I just have to get down the one set of stairs, and
then off I go. And I'm thinking about a separate entrance

right here, through the balcony. You know, building a whole new entrance ... a ramp with no stairs.

(as if to herself)

I guess I have to write to the Ministry. Write to the Ministry and request that they build it for me.

(with building confidence)

An adapted exit, an accessible exit. Some kind of form or declaration, maybe an inspection. I don't know what. But why not. I may as well try. Even if it takes forever.

(smiles)

Yeah, that'll be good. Imagine, I'll be sitting here, like, me, but eighty-five years old, just like I'm sitting here now, and – fucking hell – they'll come and say, "Anna *Alekseevna*, we have built a ramp for you!"

"Well thank you very much!"

END OF PLAY.

Photos

Russia

Figure 1 A main street in a Karelian city lined with small shops and cafés where Vera might meet an ethnographer for an interview. Several storefronts in view have an entrance with four or five steps and no access ramp. (Photo by Cassandra Hartblay)

Figure 2 and Figure 3 Apartment buildings like the one where Vakas's family might live, in early spring (left) and summer (right). Snowy, slippery streets October through April present an access barrier. (Photos by Cassandra Hartblay)

Research Process

Figure 4 In the fall of 2012, Alina and I worked together to draft her monologue for a performance about how and why poetry about Pushkin was relevant in contemporary life. Here, Alina holds the draft I had written out by hand one afternoon in her apartment. (Photo by Cassandra Hartblay)

Figure 5 and Figure 6 In the summer of 2016, we gathered in Anya's apartment to read through the Russian-language version of the script. Research participants had both critical and creative feedback for me, the ethnographer-playwright, to address and incorporate into the script. One research participant looks on and laughs as another reads from the script (left). Anya smiles to herself and drinks from a straw, as she and Rudak follow along in the script while another person reads from the script (right). (Photos by Cassandra Hartblay)

Scripting and Staging

Figure 7 Actors, playwright, and director gather backstage before the February 2016 staged reading of *I Was Never Alone* at UNC-Chapel Hill. From left to right: Meredith Kimple, Cassandra Hartblay, Germona Sharp, Daniel Doyle, Elisabeth Lewis Corley, Cuquis Robledo, and Ash Heffernan. (Photo by Cassandra Hartblay)

Figure 8 Actors Cuquis Robledo and George Barrett, playwright, and director Joseph Megel on stage during a talkback session following a February 2016 staged reading at UNC-Chapel Hill. (Photo by Cassandra Hartblay)

Figure 9 Reagan Linton (left, Phamaly Theatre) plays Vera in the October 2016 staged workshop of *I Was Never Alone* at the Shank Theatre at UC San Diego's Jacobs Theatre District/La Jolla Playhouse. In the background, Vladimir Rudak follows along in the script, between segments of the original score, which he composed and played on acoustic guitar. (Photo by Jim Carmody)

Figure 10   Jason Dorwart (UC San Diego Dept. of Theatre & Dance) plays the role of Rudak. Dorwart served as assistant director as well as performing in the October 2016 staged workshop of *I Was Never Alone* at the Shank Theatre at UC San Diego's Jacobs Theatre District/La Jolla Playhouse. He was the only cast member who had the challenge and benefit of having the person whose story his monologue is based on – the real Vladimir Rudak – in the room for rehearsals and performance. (Photo by Jim Carmody)

Figure 11 Vladimir Rudak takes center stage to perform the song "Japan" during the staged workshop performance of *I Was Never Alone* in October 2016 at the Shank Theatre at UC San Diego's Jacobs Theatre District/La Jolla Playhouse. The song, originally composed for his band, Kto Kak Mozhet, appears in the script, and in this iteration was performed by Vladimir Rudak himself. (Photo by Jim Carmody)

Figure 12 Samuel Valdez (Alternate ROOTS) performs the role of Vakas during the staged workshop performance of *I Was Never Alone* in October 2016 at the Shank Theatre at UC San Diego's Jacobs Theatre District/La Jolla Playhouse. An actor with cerebral palsy, Valdez worked extensively with director Joseph Megel (StreetSigns) to develop a speech pattern representative of the character Vakas, who has slowed speech due to traumatic brain injury, that made use of silences, pauses, and pacing for dramatic effect. (Photo by Jim Carmody)

Figure 13 and Figure 14 Irina Dubova and Judy Bauerlein face off with a rowdy scene of comedic banter as Mama and Alina in the October 2016 staged workshop at the Shank Theatre at UC San Diego's Jacobs Theatre District/La Jolla Playhouse. Dubova brought her own Soviet experiences to the role of Mama, the only character in this staging portrayed as speaking in dialect, with a Russian accent. (Photos by Jim Carmody)

Figure 15 Molly Maslak in a wistful moment during her dynamic portrayal of the character Anya in the October 2016 staged workshop at the Shank Theatre at UC San Diego's Jacobs Theatre District/La Jolla Playhouse. The table setting in front of Molly includes a bowl of clementines, a common kitchen table snack. Also visible on the table is the binder holding the playscript, from which actors during the workshop read as needed. They also followed along and read aloud some stage directions adapted for narrative accessibility during other characters' scenes. (Photo by Jim Carmody)

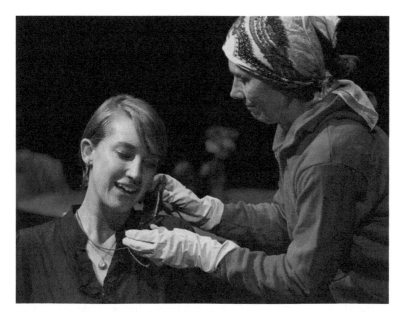

Figure 16 Production photo from the UC San Diego Fall 2016 staged workshop. The character Larissa, wearing rubber gloves, holds a cell phone while the character Anya talks into it. Molly Maslak as Anya, Judy Bauerlein (double cast as Larissa and as Alina) shown here as Larissa. (Photo by Jim Carmody)

Figure 17 Elise Morrison, staged reading director (left, standing), during rehearsal with Jason Dorwart (right, seated), playing the role of Rudak at Yale University, March 2018. (Photo by Sarah Holzworth)

Figure 18 Cassandra Hartblay introduces *I Was Never Alone* as two actors prepare to perform excerpts in a reading with musical accompaniment at the European University in Saint Petersburg in the fall of 2018, the first public reading of the script in Russian. (Photo by Anna Klepikova)

Ethnographer's Essay

Rituals of Vulnerability: Reflections on Method as Theory in Action

INTRODUCTION

I Was Never Alone is a stage play based on ethnographic research with adults with disabilities living in one Russian city. This raises several questions for readers, performers, and audiences. First, what is this genre, the ethnographic play? What does it mean to perform ethnography? Second, why is performance ethnography suitable for this particular subject matter of disability in Russia? Is there something specific about disability that calls for a performative or theatrical ethnographic engagement? Third, how does this work fit in to other projects – theatrical and ethnographic – about disability, social difference, health, and postsocialism? In this essay, I set out my own responses to the above questions, and in so doing, chart a sort of vision for the possibilities that I imagine this work opening for all of these genres.

Yet I don't think of this essay as the final word about this project. As I write these words, tucked into a home office in Toronto, Ontario, the snapshot of life represented in the script is already far off – five years ago, the time it has taken to complete the research, transcribe and process interviews, draft the script and stage readings of its various iterations, and build relationships necessary to bring this volume into being. Meanwhile, the people whose stories are adapted here have also gone on with their lives: marriages, separations, new jobs, career advances, the quiet change in self-perception that tilts across the years. While the publication of this script marks a moment of arrival at a more stable form – the imprint of ink on paper, the locking of these words into order across a longer temporal span – the play itself, *I Was Never Alone*, will continue to breathe and change, and, with each new rehearsal, performance, reading, or discussion, the work will continue to move into new cultural meanings. Like a film, the play captures one vantage point on a brief period of time, missing other angles, leaving things out (strategically or by chance), failing some expectations while meeting others. At the core, it is generative of a kind of hope for knowing about the world that hinges on a particular kind of relationship. And it is on this potentiality – the generation of a kind of relationship that I think of as ritual vulnerability that is common to ethnography, theater, and disability advocacy – that I will focus this essay.

By vulnerability, I mean a kind of openness to others. The dictionary defines vulnerability as a kind of openness to attack, injury, or wound (*OED Online* n.d.). Disability studies scholars observe that vulnerability is a shared characteristic of all human beings, yet some people are recognized as more vulnerable than others (Satz 2015; Kim 2014). Vulnerability and openness are essential to the process of knowledge production, and both ethnography and theater are ritual processes for knowledge production. In this sense, we can think of both ethnography and theater as rituals of vulnerability. And, in this essay, I argue that thinking about these ritual forms through and with disability studies insights about vulnerability enriches the practice of both.

Ethnography is the flagship methodology of the cultural anthropologist.[1] In crafting the script for *I Was Never Alone* I follow a long tradition of ethnographers who have sought opportunities to integrate creative practice into the work of ethnographic production. When an ethnographer writes for the theater, this writing comes into being not only with the intention of being *read* but also of being performed. Performance, as a mode of communication, requires relational properties of social being – the planning and staging of a production, the collaborative discussion of how to represent life on stage, the unique coeval temporality of audience-performer dynamics, and the embodied properties of acting as a mode of representation. Theater, as a kind of human activity, is a deeply ritualized social happening: audiences enter the theater, experience a symbolic performance, and leave somehow changed. I have, through the development of this play, found performance ethnography to be a productive provocation for exposing some of the core concerns facing ethnography of disability and ethnography of postsocialism. And I have observed that the work of producing performance ethnography that represents disability brings the concerns of performance ethnography, particularly the collaborative interdependency of the dialogic process, into deeper relief.

I understand performance ethnography as an example of what socially engaged artists have called "living as form," that is, as a *design* for creative practices that shifts the expectations and possibilities for human interactions. Performance ethnography, then, might be thought of as a model for engaging with experiences across difference, that, when enacted, configures the social otherwise (Escobar 2018; Hartblay, Hankins, and Caldwell 2018). Theater, research, ethnography, and performance each constitute a kind of extraordinary circumstance: an unusual manner of being and making together. As performance ethnography scholar D. Soyini Madison (2012, 10–11) holds, there is no ethnographer without the relationship of being present in the scene of fieldwork, in dialogue with interlocutors. That is, the ethnographer is not standing outside of culture looking in, but rather is participating in multiple simultaneous social worlds; there is no outside of culture. Ethnography in this view is one cultural form, a ritual for human interaction and understanding human difference, in which the ethnographer is a *coperformer*. In this way, the *practice* of ethnographic knowledge production, the *process* of interpreting and sharing meaning, rather than a subsequent text-as-object, *is* the *intended outcome*. This object that you are perhaps holding in your hand, or scrolling through, is a text that presents particular modes of intersubjective interaction, but performance ethnography is not a text – it is the proliferation of social worlds and coeval intersubjective grounds produced through the process that brought the text into being, and it is the social worlds that proliferate as this text moves forward in its next lives in book and digital text form.

I Was Never Alone or Oporniki, specifically, is both a work of performance ethnography and one part of a broader ethnographic study of disability in Northwestern Russia in the second decade of the twenty-first century. Disability, although often encountered in daily life as a taken-for-granted universal category, is deeply culturally contingent.

Anglophone readers will be most familiar with a Euro-American concept of disability. This concept of disability hinges on a series of assumptions about sociopolitical organization such as a centralized nation-state and rule of law, and on a variety of suppositions about the individual personhood, embodiment, and productivity (Ingstad and Whyte 1995). While these foundational assumptions are rooted in Euro-American cultural paradigms, the concept of disability has been widely disseminated through global governance organizations such as the World Health Organization and the United Nations and therefore impacts the way that disability advocacy unfolds across a variety of global contexts (Meekosha and Soldatic 2011). In order to parse the nuances of disability in global context, it can be useful to divide up a discussion in terms of (1) identity and subjectivity of those managing embodied identities, and (2) technologies and policies that flow globally (Ingstad and Whyte 2007, 2). By this rubric, I Was Never Alone represents "Part 1" of a larger study: the personal life history narratives in this play are essentially oral history interviews adapted for performance that may be read as a study of how my interlocutors manage disability identity in the context of life in a regional Russian city during Putin's reconsolidation of power. While writing and developing the play, I have also been at work on an ethnographic monograph that draws on the same research and could be understood as a kind of "Part 2" – a study of the ways that technologies of governance and designed technologies related to disability and disability access move transnationally and appear in the post-Soviet world of my interlocutors. So in this way, one might read I Was Never Alone as an oral history of disability experience in a particular time and place.

I also situate I Was Never Alone as *disability anthropology*. Disability anthropology, in my definition, refers to research in which disability is not only a subject matter for study but also is a kind of vantage point from which to theorize broader questions of sociological concern: personhood, redistribution, moral life, and care.[2] I distinguish disability anthropology from anthropology of disability: the former constitutes a theoretical and methodological perspective, while the latter describes merely the subject matter of research (Hartblay 2020). Significantly, disability anthropology is distinct from medical anthropology in that it frequently considers not a particular disability diagnosis (e.g., Young 1995; Cohen 1998) but the work that the word *disability*, its social construction, or social effects *do* in a given context (e.g., Kohrman 2005; Addlakha 2020). Like many ethnographers, I am interested in the ways that local, emic concepts (for instance, the Russian word *invalid*) interact with global or transnational categories that start off as normative sociological or public policy terminology, and become instrumental in the way that people make claims about resources and rights in daily life (e.g., Merry 2006; Ingstad and Whyte 2007).

In this essay, and in my broader ethnographic research on disability in Russia, I propose what I call a *relational-performative concept of disability*. This point of view expands Alison Kafer's (2013) notion of relational disability and puts it in conversation with Madison's (2012) discussion of the relational and dialogic unfolding of performance ethnography. In thinking through the relational, I draw on Victor Turner's (1988) consideration of performance to consider both social performance – the way that scholars might consider behaviors in daily life through the lens of performance – and cultural performance – those performances that are part of broader cultural processes, events, and rituals. This is not necessarily a novel approach to disability, but rather a way of naming the specific approach to disability that this work employs, building on existing scholarship. "Disability," writes Rosemarie Garland-Thomson (1997, 12–13), "[is] not so much a property of bodies as a product of cultural rules about what bodies should be or do." The nondisabled person, looking at or interacting with someone with a visible disability, struggles to see past the disability, so that "disabled people must learn to manage relationships from the beginning. In other words, disabled people must use charm, intimidation, ardor, deference, humor, or entertainment to relieve nondisabled people of their discomfort." In this way, then, social performance matters for people with disabilities, for it is through social interactions and semiotic self-expression that their personhood and citizenship might be recognized by nondisabled interlocutors (Hartblay 2020). The shift between modalities is a performative embodiment of the relational characteristics of a capable subject. As Tanya Titchkosky (2011, 45) writes, "Disability signifies something that is just enough unlike others so as to secure a unique version of help and just enough like others to be recognized as a valid form of participation." In social encounters, disability "appears," Titchkosky writes, when the need for certain kinds of help is perceived as out of place (even while all humans at some time require help from others). The performance of a disability identity in social dramas also takes into consideration the kinds of social positions that render disability powerful or denigrating. Disability is a representational category that works as part of interlocking systems of oppression, and cannot be disentangled from those relations of power (Garland-Thomson 2011, 18–20; Erevelles 2011). Furthermore, while the concept of "disability" is mobilized in liberatory struggles, not all communities have access to the concept of disability pride that has been so central to disability rights movements that laid the groundwork for Euroamerican disability theory, which some argue assumes whiteness and white-collar class status (Bell 2010; Erevelles 2011; Meekosha and Soldatic 2011; Clare 2015; Kolářová 2015; Kolářová and Wiedlack 2016; Puar 2017; Ralph 2020).[3] The relational qualities of performing roles of those in need of help, helper, or competent citizen demonstrate how disability as a concept comes into being through relationships between people, negotiating categories and care.

One challenge of this project is that in working between theater, disability studies, anthropology, and Slavic or Russian area studies there emerges a certain problem of interdisciplinarity. In particular, this problem emerges in terms of what we think of when we use the word culture, a word that is used quite differently across these epistemological spaces. In Euroamerican disability studies, the phrase *disability culture* has been deeply important for cultivating a relationship between liberatory scholarship produced in the academy and attention to the daily lived experiences of people with disabilities, disability activist traditions, and the expressive culture that disabled people and their allies produce that counters dominant ableist media narratives of disability. In this usage, disability culture refers to the situated knowledge that produces a sense of shared identity between people with disabilities and, in turn, generates *disability arts*, that is, artistic works and communities led by and centering the voices, experience, and unique expertise of people with disabilities. This concept of disability culture emerges out of a sociological and cultural theory approach to understanding disability in social life; it is deeply concerned with media and representations of disability in mainstream culture, and understanding disability as a minority culture in a complex society (Barnes and Mercer 2001). There is a long-standing scholarly debate about this inherent tension between culture in the anthropological sense and disability culture as a potentially universal concept developed in disability advocacy and disability studies (Scheer 1994; Ingstad and Whyte 1995; Brannon 1995, 9; Peters 2000; Brown 2002). This debate is complicated by the fact that disability rights and disability justice movements in the Euroamerican contexts are self-professed social movements that intentionally seek to change the dominant culture. Rather than suggest that disability culture refers to a simple liberal politics of minority recognition and intersectional identity, many disability studies scholars argue that it is possible to understand the phrase in terms of a more complex notion of culture, including how disabled people create and pass on shared, changing semiotic knowledge (Gill 1995, 18; Kuppers 2014a, 2014b). From an anthropological perspective, however, some might argue that there may be many particular disability subcultures, but that disability culture per se cannot be a universal culture in the sense of shared, symbolic, passed-on worldviews and practices. Alternatively, disability studies might be understood to be engaged in the project of mapping global disability cultures (Barnes and Mercer 2001, 528; Priestley 2001). Even so, critical global disability studies should look not only at the cultural worlds in which people with disabilities live as an object for study but also at global configurations of power in relation to disability (Grech 2015, 2016). By the same turn, *disability culture* and *disability arts* as defined above could be viewed by anthropologists tracking global frictions as folk terms of Euroamerican disability advocacy movements (see, for example of this usage, Garland-Thomson 2017, xvi). With this interdisciplinary confluence in mind, it is important to note that this essay does not describe Russian disability culture in the sense of analyzing representations of disability in high culture or pop culture, nor does it offer a survey of cultural works created by people with disabilities in Russia;[4] on the other hand, *I Was Never Alone* does document life history vantage points on contemporary Russian culture as experienced by people with disabilities who participated in the project.

In this essay, I first situate the stakes of this particular project in terms of the study of disability in contemporary Russia and then review the definition of performance ethnography and its relationship to anthropological knowledge production. With this background about performance ethnography, disability, and Russia in place, I reflect on the insights that the collaborative process of bringing *I Was Never Alone* to the stage has uncovered about the representation of contemporary Russia and of disability. Synthesizing these ideas, I suggest that performance ethnography offers a kind of ritual process for exposing vulnerabilities and building the kinds of interdependencies that facilitate the production of embodied knowledges. Performance does things that text alone cannot.

BACKGROUND

Doing Disability Anthropology in Russia

Thinking about disability in Russia requires understanding the historical context in which people make sense of the world around them and the political possibilities available. In the course of the play, characters often contrast their own perceptions of Euro-American disability advocacy strategies with the possibilities available to them in post-Soviet Russia. The way that the characters perform disability as an identity makes sense in relation to the historical, social, political, and economic context. In this way, it is important to think about the specificities of postsocialist Russia as a place and sociopolitical world in which disabled people fashion themselves as subjects. Therefore, in order to contextualize the experience of the narrators of the stories represented in the script of *I Was Never Alone*, we need a bit of context about disability and segregation in the former Soviet Union.[5]

Like the US, the USSR sought to build a new society based on scientific modernity. This meant the medicalization and pathologization of people's bodies. Soviet citizens describe a near-total lack of popular representations of disability from the 1920s to the 1970s, with a brief exception for stories and films about veterans in the years immediately following World War II.

Disability was understood as resulting from exploitation and social ills of capitalism, and so officially disability didn't exist in the Soviet Union. When a reporter asked a spokesperson for the USSR if they would mount a Paralympic team in 1980, the spokesperson famously replied: "We have no invalids in the USSR" (Phillips 2011,

1). Of course, there were many people with all kinds of disabilities and differences. Schools and sheltered workshops for the blind and deaf were developed regionally. But anecdotal historical evidence suggests that most lived at home with parents, rarely going out, or, were incarcerated in state-run institutions (Kikkas 2001; Iarskaia-Smirnova 2001; Phillips 2011).

In the 1990s, following the collapse of the Soviet Union, Western discourse about Russia has produced a powerful hegemonic narrative that described Soviet models of social welfare, education policies, and medical technologies as persistently inferior to Western (Euro-American) models. Civil society, health care, private property, real estate, financial credit and social subsidies, models of employment and economic planning, education, and the welfare state were continuously renegotiated according to this lens of transition or development toward free markets and liberal democracy. In Northwestern Russia, throughout the 1990s, programs for the professionalization of social workers and teachers, with training from abroad, introduced ideas about inclusive education, whereas all special education in the Soviet Union was segregated. And, democratization programs aimed at building civil society funded disability advocacy groups for kids with disabilities and their parents. In this context people with disabilities worked to manage perceptions of disability as a stigmatizing that indicated poverty and marginalization in popular imagination and attitudes of nondisabled post-Soviet citizens (Iarskaia-Smirnova 2001).

This immediate post-Soviet period shifted into a new phase of political reconsolidation with Vladimir Putin's re-ascendance to the presidency of the Russian Federation.[6] From 2008 on, Putin has sought to reconsolidate power centrally in the federal apparatus, and, through a variety of geopolitical actions, to break from the post–Cold War order that placed Russia as perpetually behind the West.[7] By the time I was conducting my fieldwork in 2012, the reconsolidation of federal control was well underway, and funding for grassroots NGOs serving the disability community that had been plentiful in Petrozavodsk since the 1990s had dried up. Instead, new funding possibilities opened through government channels, just as a new generation of social workers, teachers, and psychologists who hardly remembered the Soviet Union came of age and entered their professions.

When it comes to disability, in Russia today difference is still individualized as deviance, and the model of psychosocial rehabilitation prescribes work on the pathologized subjects whose bodies bear markers of disability rather than on the social structures that produce disability as difference. As Galmarini-Kabala has shown (2016), the Soviet model of disability never reconciled the state welfare model of a universal social right to human provisioning with a civil rights model of citizens advocating for political power. These two modes of disability self-advocacy existed side by side in the Soviet Union and continue to exist today. Ethnographic research in post-Soviet Ukraine suggests that disabled citizens in the post-Soviet context pick up and make use of different models of citizenship as they become useful for them (Phillips 2011; Petryna 2002). In my ethnographic research, I found that people with disabilities enacted performances of citizenship through discourses of social and civil rights and, through something akin to what Tomas Matza (2009, 2018) has called the therapeutic subject. But understanding disability as a term that can be made meaningful in the ways that it is used in daily life, that is, as a relational concept, requires thinking about the ways in which disability does not only symbolize a lack or a difference.

We Were Never Alone: Words for Disability

The play has a double title, *I Was Never Alone or Oporniki*, a convention that echoes an occasional stylistic trend that works in Russian (e.g., *The Irony of Fate, or Enjoy Your Bath* [*Ironia Sudby ili S Lyokhim parom*]), and also to gesture to the double life of this script as both a Russophone and an Anglophone text.

The phrase "I was never alone" in the title of the play comes from Alina's exchange with her mother, the character Mama. When Mama tells the audience that Alina was often left home alone as a child, Alina disagrees and responds that she was never alone, she always had a lot of people around her. Alina's actual words in Russian, "*Ya ne odinokaya*," are somewhat different. A direct translation might be, "I am not lonely," but the phrase could also mean, "I am not alone," or "I am not the only one (like this/of my kind)." For the sake of the English-language performance, I have used "I was never alone" because it best captures the sentiment in the flow of dialogue. But there is also a deeper resonance with Alina's concern with the perception that as a person with a disability, she was often alone or lonely.[8] In many representations of disability, both popular and scholarly, disabled people are represented as isolated, set apart from society, and lonely. In some cases, people with disabilities[9] really are marginalized, or denied access to forms of intimacy, or control over their own social lives;[10] in contrast, the characters in this play, based on the people with whom I conducted this ethnographic research, are more like the deaf people in Michele Friedner's (2015) monograph, seeking autonomy and intimacy, but in no way without sociality.[11] For a disabled person to correct the missive that she spent much of her childhood alone and lonely is to speak candidly against powerful systems of compulsory able-bodiedness[12] that persistently link disability and social exclusion.

I chose the secondary title, *Oporniki*, because I like the strangeness of its various possible meanings in Russian. As a medicolegal term, *invalid-opornik* implies someone with a disability related to a musculoskeletal condition, or the capacity to move freely. This category generally is the one that would encompass or describe the "type" of disabilities that people in this play have. And indeed, in the course of fieldwork, I came to know all of them in part because of social networks that were created out of educational and social services programming to target this "type" of disability.[13]

Yet it is rare to actually use the word *opornik* to describe a person with a disability in spoken Russian. Much more frequently, in daily conversation and in popular media, Russians use the word *invalid* (pronounced differently from the English "invalid" and derived from a nineteenth-century German term for injured war veterans, the word does not carry the negative connotation of "in valid" that the English "invalid" conveys). *Invalid* is the category that describes the Soviet, and now Russian, social service system equivalent to disability services and pensions in English. I have only one or two instances of it in all of my recorded interviews, so the word is an obscure one. More generally, *opornyi*, as an adjective, can mean *structural, giving strength, supporting*, or *of or related to a backbone*. So in this sense, *opornik* can also mean one who supports; one who holds things together; a source of strength; provider of structure. This definition of *opornik* is perhaps most commonly used in Russian to describe a soccer position: the role known as defensive midfield or "stopper" in English. This player acts as the backbone of the team, with the essential strength and flexible capacity to turn the course of play from defensive to offensive in a critical zone of the field.

I like this idea of people with disabilities as *oporniki*, then: by intentionally shifting this metaphorical extension of "core" or "backbone" into social relations, and thinking of people with disabilities as *oporniki* in the sense of the soccer position, we might reenvision disability not as a lonely fate, but following Alina's assertion that "there were always people around me" we might rather imagine people with disabilities (these characters, or otherwise) as supporting and holding up those around them. We can imagine the *invalidi-oporniki* at the center of each of the portraits in the play as a strong point in social relationships, as uniquely skilled in strengthening interdependencies. This is a very different understanding of the so-called structural position of disability in classical sociological theory that understands disability as a stigmatized difference, whose bearers occupy a marginal position.

Repurposing *oporniki* in this way reframes disability as a unique capacity (both structural and learned) to build relationships of interdependency and care. In making this observation, that disability and care are closely intertwined, I follow important work in feminist anthropology and disability studies. Feminist scholarship since the twentieth century has established an important critique of the idea that to need *care* is to be weak (dependent), and furthermore, that care work is not "really" work, or is often underpaid low-prestige labor. Vulnerability in Euro-American society is a feminized trait, devalued and produced as weakness in a patriarchal social order. Moreover, feminist disability anthropologists have called for attention to the unique kinship intimacies produced through disability (Friedner 2015; Ginsburg and Rapp 2001, 2011, 2013; Phillips 2011). Like the notion of deaf gain (Davidson 2016; Bauman and Murray 2010, 2014), rethinking *oporniki* centers the possibility of imagining disability otherwise, not only as synonymous with "weak" and "alone." Instead, by requiring its bearers to build nonnormative interdependencies and kinship relations (like Anya's roommate, or Vakas's digital worlds, or Alina's comedy-driven intergenerational friendship with her mother) disability calls a variety of social worlds into being, and as the *oprnik*, the central strength bearing apparatus of social worlds, holds them up. Similar to the idea of care networks between disabled folks (Piepzna-Samarasinha 2018), thinking of people with disabilities as *oporniki* situates interdependency as an innovation and strength unique to the disability community. In this play, the social relations of care are multidirectional and reciprocity between characters is uneven; yet, as foundational anthropological theory would have it, reciprocity strengthens social bonds.

To imagine disability as a source of strength and social interconnection is in direct contradiction to the typical ways in which disability appears in theatrical representations. In many plays in the Western canon, it is understood that disability should not "appear" unless it has a purpose in the overall narrative (Fox and Lipkin 2011; Sandahl 1999, 2000). Like Chekov's pistol, if a disability appears on stage, the audience should be sure that it serves a narrative purpose that will emerge in the course of the play.[14] This means that there is a very strong bias toward *compulsory able-bodiedness* (as Alison Kafer and Robert McRuer have suggested we refer to such biases generally): characters (aside from those mild impairments connoting a personality trait or type: the aged, or the professor who wears glasses) are not disabled unless there is a "reason" to be (a situation which hardly reflects the equanimity of disability in daily life). In contrast, theater scholar Dorwart (2017) argues that when disability does appear, very frequently, in the course of the play, the disabled character is either cured or dies – there you go, plot! Disability theater-makers are constantly on the lookout for new works that avoid this *curative imaginary* (to borrow a phrase from Alison Kafer 2013, 27; see also, Kim 2017, 7–9). Instead, claiming disability theater involves claiming an esthetic project for disability culture (in the disability studies sense) that plays out in the theater (Fox and Lipkin 2011; Galloway, Nudd, and Sandahl 2007; Lewis 2000).

Disability in this play is not just sad. Disability is not a tragedy. How could it be, in documentary form? It is a circumstance of daily life. Disability, by virtue of the research project at hand, is the central thread that connects the lived experiences of the narrating main characters of the play. Significantly, what ultimately connects their experiences is not a diagnosis, but rather, a shared experience of encountering the attitudes of nondisabled toward their own respective performative, bodily selves. In their own way, each character negotiates disability as a relational performance, marked by an adept virtuosity in performing vulnerability as strength.

Performance Ethnography and the Practice of Anthropology

Performance is characterized by a fleetingness of being together in time and space (Fischer-Lichte, Mosse, and Arjomand 2014). A performance is a kind of communicative moment; happenings in shared time and space demand meaningful interpretation. A shared sense of meaning depends on the interpretive capacities of cultural symbols, drawing on and produced through rituals of social communication. Performance is made meaningful by culture, and in turn shapes culture: performances affect the styles and sentiments of performers and audiences moving forward. Performance is presence together, acting together, reacting together, interpreting together. The shared process of meaning-making makes each of us anew.

Theater, as represented behavior, is deeply entwined with cultural practices of memory-making and embodied recognition of the past (Carlson 2003). Even imperfect and unfinished performances produce real effects in the social world. This is a tenuous and vulnerable process: as anyone who has performed even in a school play can attest, taking the stage to perform a role is a deeply vulnerable process. The ritual of theatrical performance breaks from the usual rules of interaction and social order, putting actor and audience together in time. An actor's stage fright hovers as a kind of anxiety about what might happen when the performance concludes, and the audience's interpretation surfaces outside of the frame of the theatrical event.

In the process of theater-making normative systems of sociality are suspended (between audience and actor, actor and director, actor and playwright, between two actors, between symbolic space and reality), and a ritualized collaborative project of creation ensues. As anthropologist Victor Turner (1982, 93) observed of performance studies scholar Richard Schechner's theatrical rehearsal process, participants in theater-making – cast, crew, director, actors – not only create some form that mimics social life, but, in fact, social performance and theatrical performance are intertwined, and the theatrical rehearsal process creates something entirely new, not only on stage, but in life. Performance and ethnography, both, then are a kind of ritual vulnerability – a design for social interaction that makes us vulnerable to one another in unusual ways. By this, I mean that both follow performative scripts with defined roles, processes, and symbolic referents.[15] Both ethnography and theater are ritualized designs for human interaction.

Performance ethnography as a term designates a methodological approach to doing ethnography that blends the ethnographic methods familiar to anthropologists, sociologists, gender studies scholars, and others with theory and practice of performance studies. This means that performance ethnography is at once interested in (1) theatrical expressive forms as a potential field site; (2) in paying attention to the performative in daily life; and (3) in engaging theatrical and performative modes of communication as an output of ethnographic research (Madison 2012; Conquergood 2013).[16] In relation to this final point, performance ethnography is especially committed to drawing out the dialogic nature of research processes; if all performance is a kind of communication, performing ethnographic research is an opening for exchange between and amongst the performance's creator(s) and audience(s). Performance ethnography holds that ethnography itself is a kind of performance. Doing ethnography involves the choreography of researcher and research participant bodies in time and space, and an attention to how research participants enact lived strategies and "establish their own politics of the body" (Cox 2015, 27–9). Moreover, because of the emphasis on *the body* in performance, performance ethnography draws out "the kinetic values or *doing* of ethnographic research, it charges the activism nascent in putting one's body on the line" both in terms of the body's relationship to making texts, to acting or moving on stage, or to doing fieldwork (Pollock 2006, 325). In this tradition, doing performance ethnography is a radical act, predicated on, hinging on, and made meaningful by a drive to employ the process of coperformance to serve the cause of justice.

Written ethnography and ethnographic performance differ in important ways. Ethnography as a written genre directly states theoretical ideas based on the author's analysis of ethnographic material – whether quotations from interviews, observations, or images. The authority of text fixes the ethnographer's interpretive point of view at a given point in time in print.[17] Readers consider that text at a later date, usually without reading the author's words aloud or directly encountering the author, but often interpreting meaning in concert with one another (e.g., in the classroom).[18] In contrast, performance is never fixed, or even replicable. No two rehearsals or performances are exactly alike. The composition of audience, the conditions of the performance location, the mood of the performers, and myriad other variables come together in a unique event (Fischer-Lichte et al. 2014). In performance, meaning emerges through autopoietic feedback between audience and performers unfolding in shared space and time. When developing ethnographic performance, in contrast to the process typical in developing written ethnography, the ethnographer's interpretation is worked out collaboratively and often out loud with research participants, performers, production staff (theater director, dramaturg, set and lighting design, etc.), and audience members – both independently and in concert. New analyses and insights emerge with each new process reading, rehearsal, and performance. Moreover, memories of performances past and the possibility of future performances make any writing about works of performance deeply inchoate.

The style of performance ethnography engaged in the making of *I Was Never Alone* is part of a scholarly lineage following the writings of Dwight Conquergood, an ethnographer who worked primarily out of the School of Communication at Northwestern University in the late twentieth century (Johnson 2013; Madison 2006) and has been taken up elsewhere, largely in performance studies programs. Simultaneously, Richard Schechner at New York University, in collaboration with Victor and Edith Turner, established a separate and influential school of performance studies, which employs ethnography in the work of decentering the European canon in the history of theater and explores how theatrical and performance processes play different roles in enacting social processes in different cultural settings (Schechner 2004). Both of these complementary performance studies traditions now claim as common (and quite different) ancestors Erving Goffman's consideration of performance in everyday life, and Zora Neale Hurston's theatrical writing.[19] Yet this performance ethnography tradition has remained somewhat distinct from conversations in the anthropological canon.

The concept of performance ethnography loops back through lineages of anthropological discourse. The Conquergood school of performance ethnography builds on anthropologist Johannes Fabian's scholarship. In particular, Fabian insists that one inexorable element of the anthropological project of ethnography is the hoped-for practice of being together in time, and the risk of placing our interlocutors in another temporal or asynchronous frame (Pandian 2012, 549; Fabian 1983/2014, 31). Conquergood (2006) extended Fabian's notion of the coeval moment. For Fabian (1983/2014, 42), the interchange of coevalness, being-together-in-time, that is shared between ethnographer and research subject is a defining characteristic of the ethnographic encounter, in that "Time, in the sense of shared, intersubjective Time, is a necessary condition of communication." Fabian (2014) argued that it is through a disjuncture in shared temporal communality, or coevalness, that the ethnographer is able to distance the research subject as an "other" – leaving the field site and the engagement of the ethnographer in the research participants' own temporal world, the ethnographer creates an "other" in the image of the research subject by a retelling of the fieldwork in a temporal order that excludes the research subject. Fabian (1990, 4–5) writes, "Although [anthropologists] do our field research on the premise of coevalness, of sharing time with our interlocutors on equal terms, we then go on to produce an allochronic discourse based on temporal distancing; we construct an Other whom we relegate to times other than our own." Moreover, the other is represented as somehow living in the past, rendered temporally distant through idiomatic labels like *tribal*, *primitive*, and *underdeveloped* (Conquergood 2006, 354). Conquergood (2006, 360–1) argues for other disciplines to emulate the anthropological turn away from the authority of the text toward "the performance paradigm as an alternative to the atemporal, decontextualized, flattering approach of text-positivism," as exemplified by Victor Turner's work on theater in the 1980s.

Furthermore, Conquergood (2006) understands ethnographers and interlocutors as collaborators in a performative interaction. This formulation, which he calls *coperformance*, leaves behind hierarchies of colonial knowledge production (the scholar and the studied). D. Soyini Madison (2006) writes:

> Performance demands that the researcher's body must be cotemporally present and active in a dialogical meeting with the Other – this is co-performance ... For Conquergood, "[participant] observation" connotes an arrogance of seeing and judgement that co-performance refutes in its being and doing with the Other in a more intersubjective and interpersonal engagement. (349)

In this way, the ethnographic praxis prescribed by contemporary North American performance studies is distinct from but deeply in dialogue with the ethnography practiced in socio-cultural anthropology.

As ethnographers we perform the role of the listener or recorder, we perform the act of participation, of writer. In this way, performance ethnography means to conceptualize ethnographic practice as an intersubjective, collaborative process (Conquergood 2013; Fabian 2000). Fabian (1990, 7) wrote, "The ethnographer's role [is] no longer that of a questioner; he or she is but a provider of occasions, a catalyst in the weakest sense, and a producer (in analogy to a theatrical producer) in the strongest." That is, Fabian suggested, that the act of ethnographic research, decoupled from a positivist project, is a design for a particular kind of human action or interaction.

At the same time that performance ethnography calls for its practitioners to locate ethnography as a kind of cultural performance, it recognizes the liminal capacity of performance to change its participants: audience, producers, performers, and directors are all transformed through performance. Moreover, performance ethnography shifts the organization of social relations in its very process of coming into being.[20] "Performance," writes Diane Conrad (2012, 16), "creates opportunities for communion among participants, researchers, and research audiences." The ethnographer conducting performance ethnography is no longer alone in the production and interpretation of knowledge, but rather participating in a collaborative process. The ethnographer, research participants, production designers, performers, and audience members participate in (or in various ways, *resist* participation in) a ritual process of becoming otherwise together. In doing so, they release control over how the process will end, opening to the vulnerability of becoming together.

While I trace a particular lineage behind the performance ethnography praxis that I studied and deployed in making *I Was Never Alone*, the definition of performance ethnography is not set but negotiated and changing: practitioners of performance ethnography have observed the manifold ways in which performance and ethnography might intersect, and they have developed a wide array of projects employing performance ethnography methods. Performance ethnography, though, should be differentiated from documentary theater based on ethnographic research; even as performance ethnography evolves as a praxis, a core defining element is that it entails a dialogic process in which the research continues through the work of performance. For example, Magdalena Kazubowski-Houston (2015) coauthored a play script with her research participants – a group of ethnic minority women in Poland – and documented the process of developing the script and staging the play so that the conflicts and drama that emerged in the process of crafting that performance became the subject for her ethnography, published in a monograph alongside the script. That is, *I Was Never Alone* represents just one manner by which ethnographers might engage performance, following the format of adapting interview transcripts into a script for performance.[21]

In anthropological practice today, there are other ways to engage theatrical performance in ethnographic practice that do not follow the performance ethnography model. For instance, Cristiana Giordano and Greg Pierotti, working in collaboration as anthropologist and documentary theater director, have developed a new method for working with performance as part of the work of ethnographic analysis. Unlike the performance ethnography project described here, which centers the work of developing a script as a text, their technique, called *affective devising*, uses empirical research and theater prompts in a studio environment to create "narrative and non-narrative structures" for understanding fieldwork experiences (Giordano and Pierotti 2017). Giordano and Pierotti (2017) suggest that embodied performance of concepts from fieldwork allows the interpreting researcher/performer to engage in "non-representational theory." Bodily performance is at once doing *and* interpreting, representing *and* drawing lyrical connections. Rather than performing ethnographic findings in a realist style, Giordano and Pierotti use experimental and nonrepresentational performance to work through conceptual problems suggested by ethnographic encounters.

Broadly speaking, these quite different approaches to integrating performance practice into the work of doing ethnography are often grouped together under the umbrella of "experimental" ethnographic practice, method, or methodology. Yet this formulation fails to capture the ways in which sociocultural anthropology's interpretive turn in the 1970s (Geertz 1973) and subsequent "crisis of representation" in the 1980s (Clifford and Marcus 2010; Kazubowski-Houston 2015, 115) suggested the profoundly experimental, situated, and contingent quality of all ethnographic knowledge production. In this vein, rather than think of performance ethnography as "experimental," it is perhaps more accurate to call it one of a variety of *imaginative* or *creative* ethnographic methodologies (Elliott and Culhane 2017). This follows in some ways the development of traditions of praxis known as research-creation, qualitative inquiry (as exemplified by the journal of that name), participatory research (Parker et al. 2017), sensory ethnography (Pink 2015), and visual anthropology. All of these various practices of knowledge production intentionally step away from positivist traditions and toward practices that disengage from writing as the primary modality in the broader ethnographic practice of coming to know through creation.

Perhaps the one vein in which the "experimental" moniker continues to apply is in terms of pedagogy and labor. The field of sociocultural anthropological training at the doctoral level often assumes that PhD students already know how to do ethnography. The majority of our practitioners think, play, and experiment with interpretation through the medium of the written word, and where methods courses are offered in sociocultural anthropology departments, they necessarily foreground these practices as the core of the discipline – after all, who are sociocultural anthropologists if not those who do fieldwork in order to write ethnographies? In this way, creative methods are experimental in that they are contingent, alone out there on a limb in a given department, and, in no way have we exhausted the possibilities for what written ethnography can do. The work of doing performance ethnography, like visual anthropology, requires a particular skill set and artistic practice, often requires developing collaborators, and sometimes, as with visual anthropology, requires asking one's interlocutors for different kinds of engagement and consent for different kinds of representation. The labor of making performance is profoundly different from the labor of making texts. Yet, as many others have observed, the practice of writing, the making of texts, is also "experimental": it is a process of discovery by which something is worked out.[22]

Disability Theater and Performance Ethnography

If performance ethnography is one method for attending to subjugated knowledges and putting the body on the line, to what extent is performance ethnography engaged with disability studies? How does thinking with critical disability studies shift or shape the aesthetics and commitments of performance ethnography? Performance studies and disability studies have a long and productive mutual engagement (Henderson and Ostrander 2010; Sandahl and Auslander 2005). Ethnographic work by anthropologists working in conversation with these fields has emerged recently (Dokumaçi 2016, 2017; Scott 2014). Disability studies scholars have developed a great deal of scholarship regarding disability theater, that is, documenting theater practices and works that can be understood as examples of disability arts and disability culture (as defined above) (Johnston 2016, 1). Yet there is little work in anthropology or performance ethnography that might be read as ethnography of disability theater or as performance ethnography that is also disability anthropology. However, performance studies accounts of disability theaters do employ ethnographic modalities to describe performances and performance development processes (e.g., Fox and Lipkin 2011) and performance studies considerations of tropes of disability make use of autoethnographic forms (e.g., Henderson 2006).

A disability studies approach to theater first observes the compulsory able-bodiedness implicit in mainstream North American theater. Practitioners and audiences are frequently presumed to be able-bodied, and access needs or bodily and sensory differences are produced as always exceptions to the norm (Johnson 2012). Projects that center disabled bodies or intentionally bring together diverse audiences to participate in a shared ritual of theater (thereby changing the form of the ritual itself) tend to be understood as marginal, experimental, or "new" (e.g., relaxed theater). Petra Kuppers (2017) argues that feeling at ease in the theater is a privilege of nondisabled people. She writes:

> Disability as a lived category can hardly ever afford that distance from the realities of bodies and their fit or non-fit with social space. We have to think about how to get into the theatre, how to get into our seat, how to access the spectacle – these are core issues for disabled audiences. For disabled performers, some central questions are: How do I get on to the stage? Is the dressing room accessible? Are there scripts that have space for me? Are there casting directors that can make use of my particular talents without casting me only as an elder or an outsider? (5)

In this vein, a disability studies approach to theater makes a second observation: that by being in the theater and doing theater disabled people transform the politics and poetics of the embodied practice.

Disability theater, then, like other disability arts practices, centers the creative work of people with disabilities and integrates an ethos of disability access into the production process. Following the disability culture and disability arts model, disability theater is not only theater about disability but also theater that centers the expertise of people with disabilities and the practices of accessibility that make that leadership possible. For instance, practitioners have documented a special relationship between disability theater and documentary theater. The aesthetic tradition of one-man shows in confessional, memoir, and comedic style has played an important role in the development of disability theater (for example, Galloway et al. 2007; Fraser 2001). Speaking in one's own voice, the one-man show presents a space for the artist to perform disability on their own terms. The one-man show centers a specific, personal point of view, building on the mission of the disability studies perspective to represent people with disabilities in their own words on their own terms (Linton 2005; Couser 2005, 2011). The aesthetic resonance of this one-man show style of disability theater reverberates in the monologue-like form of *I Was Never Alone*, demonstrating the capacity of the poetics of disability theater to be referenced through theatrical form; disability theater is recognizable not only by its subject matter.

Disability theater practitioners differentiate disability theater from simply theater that "includes" disabled people or creates work about disabled people. Following the broader concept of disability aesthetics of disability arts, disability theater is theater wherein "disability aesthetics invites us to think about disability as a desirable and celebrated way of being in the world" (Cripping the Arts 2019). Disability theater is not an additive equation (disability *plus* theater) but produces a distinctive aesthetic and a community of practice (Fox and Lipkin 2011). In particular, the problem of accessibility in theatrical practice and architectural spaces is a creative problem that produces artistic outcomes. For instance, in the case of mobility access barriers faced by practitioners with disabilities, disabled creators challenge spatial assumptions and make unexpected artistic choices that unsettle norms and produce compelling aesthetic outcomes (Lewis 2004). In one case documented by performance studies scholar Victoria Lewis, creators staged a play performance in a stairwell when the stage itself was inaccessible. Disability theater integrates an "ethos of accommodation" into the creative process, with profound impacts on the aesthetic results (Galloway et al. 2007). This foregrounding of accessibility as not only a technical problem to be solved but a resource for creative innovation is characteristic of an anti-ableist approach to the arts.

How, then, is performance ethnography as a dialogic ethnographic praxis shifted by engaging this ethos? What creative innovations might foregrounding the aesthetics of access provoke for practitioners of performance ethnography? Or, what observations about accommodation as an ethos might performing ethnographic work about disability bring to the fore? *I Was Never Alone or Oporniki* offers an opportunity to think with the disability theater ethos of accessibility and bring this to bear on the tradition of performance ethnography. Returning to the notion of *oporniki* discussed above, could disability access be reframed as a *central support* for a disability theory of performance ethnography? How might understanding *disability access as a central support* crip unexamined norms in performance ethnography praxis? These questions will not be answered through an analysis of the script's content but might be explored through ethnographic analysis of performance and the script development process.

PERFORMING INTERDEPENDENCY AND CRIP TIME ON STAGE

Meredith nods and turns to make eye contact with Ash, who is standing next to her, a yellow cleaning glove on her one hand, and a cup with a plastic bendy straw grasped in the other hand. They are standing on stage during a rehearsal, running the final scene of *I Was Never Alone*.

"I use straws a lot too," Meredith says, "so this makes sense to me."

Joseph, the director, says, "All right, so let's run the cell phone again, and then with the drinking, I think you can take even longer with the drinking."

I smile from where I am sitting in the theater, a few seats away and a row behind Joseph. That day, in February 2016, during rehearsals for the first full-staged reading of the draft script of *I Was Never Alone*, I was gunning for the performers to slow down on this stage direction, in which the character Anya, played by Meredith, calls to the character Larissa, played by Ash, and asks her to come help her to answer her phone (see Figure 16). Larissa then offers Anya a drink of water. The character Anya has a disability that makes lifting even household objects difficult, so the script includes stage directions indicating how Anya should drink with Larissa's assistance.

LARISSA: I'm going to have something to drink. Do you want something?

(*ANYA nods. LARISSA pours herself some water and drinks. She takes another cup, this one a very light, cheaply made plastic one, and adds barely a half inch of water to it from the pitcher. Still facing the counter, looking for something, LARISSA asks*)

Where's your straw?

ANYA: Katya and I rearranged things. It's by the forks.

(*LARISSA opens a drawer and takes out a pink plastic drinking straw with a bend in it, the kind you would buy in a pack for a child's birthday party. She places the straw in the cup and adjusts the bend. She turns and puts the cup in ANYA's hand. ANYA slowly raises the cup to her mouth, puts her lips around the straw, and drinks.*)

LARISSA: (*briefly*)
More?

ANYA: No, thank you.

(*LARISSA takes back the cup, rinses it quickly along with her own, and puts them back in the dish drain. She turns back to ANYA.*)[23]

Although Anya is seated in a power wheelchair throughout the scene, this is the first point in the portrait at which the audience encounters the degree to which she requires assistance in even simple personal care tasks, like drinking.

"So while she's drinking, really go ahead and check in with her," Joseph directs the actors. "Look at each other, more drinking, and then sort of, Anya, just take your time drinking until you're done." He glances back at me.

"Make sure," I chime in, "that this plays as something familiar, something you've done a million times before, that you do every day."

"Okay, again!" commands Joseph, then, flipping back a page in the script, "from 'I've had it with all these disabled people.'"

They run the segment of the scene again, this time settling in to the nonverbal communication between one character who is holding the cup and drinking straw for the other, who is drinking. In this performance Ash (Larisa) held the cup for Meredith (Anya); while the character Anya is based on a person who holds her own cup, the actress Meredith, at the time of the performance, had cups held for her.

A few days later, the reading opens with an evening performance followed by a talkback session. Meredith and Ash play the interaction deeply, beautifully, settling into the intimacy and ease of their characters' relationship. The theatrical stakes of spending several full beats on the act of drinking water – one woman in her twenties holding a straw for another – expands into the silent, shuffling theater.

After the performance, during the talkback session, a nondisabled audience member – identifying herself as a grad student in literature who has no background in disability studies – remarks that she found the moment to be extremely moving. She comments that as Anya talked, narrating her observations about social attitudes and the psychology of disability with sharp professionalism and wit, she felt herself identifying with the character. The audience member tells the crowd she felt that she and Anya shared so many experiences, although she herself has never had a disability and the character is obviously a wheelchair user. "But it wasn't until she was drinking," the audience member said, addressing the audience and the actors assembled on stage, "that I realized how different our day-to-day lives must be, and also, that if I hadn't encountered it in this way, I might have assumed that someone with disabilities like hers – that she needs help to drink – that we wouldn't have a lot in common. But the way the scene unfolded, it came the other way around." Encouraging the actors to slow down and dig into the slowness of the straw encounter opened nondisabled audience members to sitting with what disability scholars call *crip time* (Price 2011; Kafer 2013; Kuppers 2014a, 2014b; Samuels 2017), the temporal specificity of nonnormative embodiments navigating social relations with people and things.

Meanwhile, the scene offers actors with disabilities a chance to perform a representation of disability experience that locates communication in the lived experience of body rather than in the conceptual qualities of text or theory. For disabled actors, the scene segment is an example of what Ingunn Moser and John Law (1999) call *good passages*. That is, it is one of those moments when human users and their coperformers, human and otherwise, align and facilitate an experience of ease. Put another way, the drinking straw, in concert with Larissa's hand and the cup, offers a performative affordance (for more on affordances in this context, see Dokumacı 2016, 2017), a possibility that might otherwise be foreclosed if technical and relational configurations were otherwise.

Some months later, Joseph and I were in La Jolla, California, staging a longer workshop performance of the project in UC San Diego's Department of Theatre and Dance. Our cast in La Jolla was rather different from the North Carolina group. Meredith, who played Anya in North Carolina, has a disability similar to the character herself, and Ash, who played Larissa, is someone with a physical disability (she has one, not two, hands) but has an embodied sense of adaptive strategies. In contrast, in La Jolla, although we had cast actors with disabilities in most roles, by chance it happened that neither of the actors playing Anya and Larissa identified as disabled. Because Larissa is a secondary character in the play, appearing only briefly in Anya's portrait for two small exchanges, the role is double cast, that is, played by an actor playing another primary role.

During a read-through early on in the La Jolla rehearsal process, when we reached the cell phone-cup-straw exchange, Joseph asked me to explain the scene beyond the information contained in the stage direction. I explained that Larissa holds the cup for Anya because Anya herself has very little muscle strength, and lifting a cup is quite difficult for her.

This was a fact about the real person on whom the character of Anya is based that I had observed first hand during fieldwork interviews and visits to Anya's apartment. Sometimes, meeting in her kitchen, Anya would ask her housemate or a friend who was visiting, or her mother when at her parents' apartment, to pour her just a little bit of tea or water, and then she would lift the cup herself. Sometimes, she would direct me to pour something for myself and for her as well, giving very careful and deliberate instructions. As a guest at her house, I wouldn't have helped myself to tea, but her instructions about how to pour or where to find cups served as a performative indication of hospitality. Living every day in a body that did some things very well, and others not well at all, she was adept at giving instructions to others without any kind of apology.

This element of Anya's scene took a while to land during the San Diego workshop. Finally, in one rehearsal, assistant director Jason Dorwart, who uses a wheelchair and an aide for many daily tasks, interjected.

"Can I add something here?" he asked Joseph, as they paused mid-scene for commentary.

"Of course."

Jason turned to the actress playing Anya. "You have to give directions without self-pity. You're not apologizing for asking her to do something for you. You don't feel bad about it. It's how you do things. If you didn't tell other people what to do, you wouldn't be able to do anything." Jason asserted.

Later, Jason would write a short reflection on the La Jolla workshop of *I Was Never Alone* for a theater journal, asserting that the play offers an approach to depicting disability on stage that is markedly different from standard theatrical representations. He wrote:

> Because of the ubiquity of disability in our narratives, and the common assumption that disability must be a tragedy, the majority of theatrework tells stories from the perspective of the privileged and able-bodied, rather than from the perspective of disabled people themselves. Audiences are accustomed to having disability on stage elicit responses of sympathy, pity, and tragedy; and actors are conditioned to play those roles with that same attitude.

It was this customary sense of pity that the actress playing Anya had to eschew in order to portray the character from an insider's point of view. Many theater scripts and movies use disability as a symbol: a way to elicit in an audience a sense of pity. Cultural archetypes offer further tropes of disability – the blind man who can see the truth, the "Tiny Tim" character who serves to refract the moral orientation of other nondisabled characters, the physically disabled hunchback or hag whose nonnormative body type flags stigma and social isolation. It was for this reason that disability theorists have argued that in literature and other cultural representations disability acts as a kind of "narrative prosthesis," a tool to signal something else, a plot device

(Mitchell and Snyder 2001; Garland-Thomson 1997). The curative imaginary, Jason has argued in his own scholarship, goes further: it becomes a driver of otherwise flaccid plots, wherein disabled characters are either cured of disability or die (Dorwart 2017). In contrast, Dorwart argues, theater needs representations of disability in which disability is not a metaphor for anything else and not a plot device.

Talking to me after the workshop, Jason remarked that the actors with disabilities in the cast were able to "get" their roles much more quickly than the nondisabled actors. This, he said, and later wrote in his reflection piece, is why casting disabled actors is so important. Disability doesn't signify anything: it simply is.

Anya is not socially isolated. Nonnormative bodies like hers are so frequently indications for actors to play for pity, that an actress otherwise unacquainted with disability identity first had to move beyond this dominant cultural trope in order to play the character fully. Instead of social isolation, the unusual circumstances of Anya's embodiment, as she explains in her scene, have led her to build an unusual network of care around herself. Inviting a family friend to live with her in an apartment as a roommate/assistant for discounted rent, Anya improvised a kind of crip kinship, inventing a social role for which there was no obvious name.[24] At the same time, her idea for this living situation built on generations of crip cultural knowledge: the idea that adults with disabilities might establish themselves independently of their families of origin, outside of institutions, and lead professional lives and adult social lives came from Anya's wide reading in disability advocacy. The rituals of vulnerability that nonnormative embodiment requires of Anya for survival in turn require her to build relationships of reciprocity, drawing care networks tightly together. *Oporniki*, at the center of a set of social relations.

For the nondisabled performers like the actress playing Anya in San Diego, for Joseph, the director working on a disability show for the first time, and for many of the set designers, *I Was Never Alone* was a play about disability. Their journey through the rehearsal and performance was a process of undoing dominant cultural stereotypes about disability, learning to see disability not as a metaphor but as a set of performative relations, and coming to recognize the strength in vulnerability that characterizes the social embeddedness of the *oporniki* in *I Was Never Alone*. But as Reagan Linton, who played Vera in La Jolla, pointed out to me, for actors with disabilities in the show, the conundrum they faced was the problem of how to understand what it means to have a disability in *Russia*.[25] Of course, many actors were playing disabilities different from their own, and life circumstances very different from what they themselves had experienced. And so, the journey of the show was about acting in all of its rich decision-making and performative artistry: what makes a moment, how should a given line be played, which hand gesture carries the phrase. But Reagan's comment was part question: what did she need to know about Russia in order to play her character, not as the North American equivalent, but as somehow, really *Russian*?

SPOTLIGHT ON METHODS: Origins and Writing Process

In the fall of 2012, as an American anthropologist conducting ethnographic fieldwork on disability and social exclusion in Russia, I joined a group of unemployed adults with disabilities participating in an art therapy group in one city in Northwest Russia. After meeting the members of the group, I was invited to attend the group's weekly meetings and participate in their activities as a guest. After explaining my broader project, some of the participants let me know that they would be willing to be part of my book project, and I arranged to visit them at home for one-on-one interviews. All of our communication – in group, in interviews, online or over the phone to make plans – was conducted in Russian, my second language, which by this point, I had studied for over ten years and spoke nearly fluently (native speakers recognized my accent, but usually could not tell where I was from), and the native language for all of the people in this project. This was one part of my broader research on this subject, conducted over ten months that academic year, with preliminary and follow up trips in preceding and subsequent years.

Over the course of the fall, I got to know the members of the group, often riding in the van with them on the way home; simultaneously, I continued conducting research and interviews with other disability advocates and disability service groups in the region. The

art therapy group's organizers had arranged for a variety of activities in the first half of the fall – photography, drawing –
and then, not long after I began attending the weekly meetings,
the focus shifted to preparations for a culminating performance. A
local youth theater director volunteered her time to work with the
group for several weeks to help to develop a concept and script
for a performance. The members of the group didn't have much in
common other than their status as unemployed young adults with
disabilities, a common scenario for disability groups in Russia and
elsewhere. With this problem at the fore and only one meeting per
week, the group was quite limited in terms of the kind of performance that it would be possible to create.

After some discussion, the group settled on a recital of poetry
by the famous Russian poet Alexander Sergeevich Pushkin (see
Figure 4). Over the course of a few weeks, the group members were
each charged with selecting and rehearsing a "favorite" Pushkin
poem – an assignment something like assigning a group in North
America to pick and memorize and recite a favorite Shakespeare
monologue or sonnet, in the sense that Pushkin is understood as a
seminal poet of the Russian language and recitation of poetry is a
genre unto itself in Russia. The selection of Pushkin poetry was an
easy choice given that everyone already had some familiarity with
his oeuvre. But it was not without a sort of nationalist assimilationist impulse: through the performance of Pushkin, disabled interlocutors demonstrated their competence as members of the Russian
nation capable of participating in the hagiography of Pushkin as a
secular symbol of Russian national distinction. The resulting script
was formally quite traditional and, as the group leaders pointed
out, didn't offer much in the way of integrating the personal experiences of the groups' participants into the mix. Yet, even while many
of the group members did observe that the plan to simply recite
Pushkin – in some cases with costumes, dance, or musical accompaniment – was awfully elementary, or in one participant's words,
childish, no one could quite come up with a better idea. After all,
given that many of the group members were unemployed and had
mobility impairments that made the financial and physical expense

of getting out of the house especially difficult, the social experience of planning and executing the performance (and the expenses-covered accessible van ride to and from the group's meetings) was more important than the particular content of the performance. On the day of the performance, everyone dressed up a bit, performed their section, and then gathered around a celebratory table laden with fruit, cakes, chocolate, and tea. A rowdy yet chaste party ensued (sugar and caffeine only, no alcohol), which participants later looked back on fondly in interviews or written reflections that they shared with me.

But, although that autumn's program ended on a high note, I was left wondering: What would a play that told their own stories be like? It was with this question in mind that I proposed a play project to my closest interlocutors, some who had participated in the Pushkin performance, as well as to several others who were working on disability advocacy issues in the area. My interlocutors already knew that I was doing research in order to write a book about disability experience in their region, so they weren't particularly surprised by the suggestion. I explained that I had worked in the past with a theater group in the US where people with disabilities themselves participated in writing the scripts as well as performing them, and that I thought that a play might be an interesting way to reach more people and to represent what it is like to have a disability in Russia for both North American and Russian audiences. Several interlocutors were open to the idea, and I continued recording one-on-one interviews in Russian, with the thought that once back home, I would develop both a play and a dissertation simultaneously.

Proposing a play project to my collaborators in Russia was not the same as proposing such a project back home: it entered into the historical context of post-Soviet theatrical practice and popular expectations. For my interlocutors whose stories appear in the play, my proposal to write a play based on their stories was not so different than my parallel proposal to write a book. Both ideas were just another "project" proposed by one in a long line of well-intentioned visiting Americans: throughout their childhoods

they were often invited to participate in democratization programs around the city, usually funded and sometimes conducted
by visiting foreigners. There had been a project to start an online
radio program for disabled teenagers; another to train disabled
youth as citizen journalists; a summer camp; a democracy and
business initiative (from which the local coordinator still had a
suitcase of winter clothing that the visiting American had left with
her in hopes that they would be refunded and he would return
another year); and the several programs mentioned in the play.
When I explained the idea of a documentary play, using the adjective *dokumental'nyi*, the word used to contrast documentary
film with narrative film, my interlocutors seemed to know what I
meant, even though none of them had ever *seen* a documentary
play, per se.

In contrast to my interlocutors, theater practitioners in Russia
at the time had very specific ideas about what documentary, verbatim, or ethnographic theater might be. I had first learned of the
contemporary Russian documentary theater movement while
working as program coordinator at an arts nonprofit in New York in
2009 when I was tasked with arranging a staged reading of several
excerpts from new plays by young Russian playwrights. With short
scenes from Aleksandr Rodionov and Mikhail Durnenkov and others translated into English for the first time, I remember being surprised when my Russian coworkers remarked at how unusual the
plays were.[26] The subject matter – down and out Muscovites arguing at a bus stop, the cruel hazing in army barracks – seemed to me
similar to American standard fare fodder for contemporary playwriting. The plays carried the hallmark of that style of contemporary playwriting that looks hard at a tiny social world, then tries to
recreate its characters and mores – however brazen or "uncultured"
they may be – on stage. In short, this subject matter looked like a
lot of the one-act plays that had enamored us in my high school
drama club. What I didn't fully understand until years later was that
these playwrights were part of a wave of "new" Russian playwrights,
whose work had only ever existed in post-Soviet Russia, as Soviet
censorship had discouraged plays about social strife.

Sometimes referred to as "New Russian Drama," this new approach to playwriting, according to those involved, came about when a group of Moscow theater practitioners invited and hosted a series of workshops on British documentary theater: workshops sent playwrights out into the city with tape recorders to record scenes from daily life; those scenes were transcribed, and then adapted for the stage (Freedman 2014, 1–8; Serebrennikov 2009, 9–11). A play that marked the emergence of this movement was Aleksandr Rodionov's *Battle of the Moldovans for a Cardboard Box*, which staged the rambling arguments of two homeless or down-and-out men (Dugdale 2009, 16). Through these workshops, a new generation of young playwrights were exposed to documentary theater practices (a sort of strand in British theater of the time). Led by Elena Grumina and Mikhail Ugarov, theater practitioners from an older generation working to foster and support works by a new generation of playwrights, this ethnographically minded New Russian Drama found a home with the establishment of the Teatr.doc theater in a small basement space in a Moscow courtyard (15–18). Theater writers look back on this moment as heralding a shift in theatrical style:

> [When] Ugarov and Gremina sent young writers out into the field ... in a major city dominated for decades by Chekhov, Ostrovsky, and Shakespeare, a whole array of plays about miners, mothers in prison, factory workers, homeless people, and alienated teenagers began to appear. Traditionalists were horrified. Miners and prisoners don't speak a gentile form of Russian, and many believed that only gentile Russian should be spoken on stage. (Freedman 2018)

In this way, the New Russian Drama of the early 2000s that became the most well-known dramatic movement to mobilize documentary theater techniques in Russia should be understood as genealogically related to, yet conceptually and stylistically different from, the human rights and political advocacy foundations of documentary theater in Europe and the United States (Lipovetsky and Beumers 2008; Beumers and Lipovetsky 2009). Much of this work depicted violence and unsympathetic lead characters. Unlike documentary theater developed with straightforward advocacy in mind, characters in these works did not necessarily appeal to viewers' sympathies. Instead this new Russian documentary theater forced audiences to reckon with corruption, poverty, and cruelty that mainstream Soviet and contemporary theater productions shied away from. Although these plays did not take the perspective of encouraging a viewer to develop empathy for a minority group or underrepresented perspective in the liberal democratic moral register (as with some of the most well-known anglophone documentary theater, from *The Vagina Monologues* to *The Laramie Project*), the new genre did take on political tones. For instance, Teatr. doc subsequently staged verbatim transcripts of courtroom scenes entangled in overtly political debates in Putin's Russia.[27]

Once I returned to the US, where I began work writing a dissertation based on this research, I also set to work adapting some of the interview text for performance (see Appendix 1). I had an archive of over seventy interviews as digital audio files, each with a short paragraph-length description in my interview log; I transcribed or hired native-speaker research assistants to transcribe most but not all of these interviews. This archive also included notes – handwritten and typed – from hours of participant observation and informal interviews, as well as research materials related to broader public attitudes about disability, from memes to newspaper articles to legal codes and ministry website copy. Some interlocutors I interviewed again and again; others I interviewed only a few times but saw frequently; still others, referred through mutual acquaintances, I met for one interview, without follow up. In thinking through whose stories might be included in a performance, I was bound by an ethical obligation to only use those interviews that I was confident could be used with permission. This meant a combination of those interviewees with whom I was quite close and had very good rapport (the real people represented by the characters of Alina and her mother; Vakas; Sergei; Anya), and those whom I knew already had spoken publicly as disability advocates (Vera; Rudak). When I returned to Russia briefly for a follow-up trip in the spring of 2014 to see the performance of another theater project I had worked on during my fieldwork, I met with interlocutors and recorded further interviews to help fill in gaps and check that my analysis for my dissertation thus far was on track.

In the winter and spring of 2015, I enrolled in a graduate playwriting workshop, and through this experience was able to hear pages read aloud nearly every other week throughout a semester. This allowed me to experiment with many of the problems that came up in the course of adapting interview transcripts for performance: How to write each voice in translation so that the characters had distinctive patterns and manners of speech that referenced relevant anglophone tropes? How to arrange the text so that the format of an interview (and the direct address that it implies) made sense in the course of a stage play? Should I include the ethnographer as a character? Should each character have their own scene, or should scenes be arranged topically, as in a documentary film, with multivocal discussions of school, family, coming of age, and politics? The decisions that I made about these and other questions were based on my own writerly instincts and capacities, my earlier training in performance ethnography before leaving for the fieldwork, and the input of the seminar participants. By the end of the term I had a first full draft of a script, at that time, seven monologues. Over the next year, I continued to workshop the script in table readings. I made a lot of edits: adding additional characters to each scene, cutting down the length of each scene, and generally working to improve the impact of the writing for performance.

Looking back on this period, the work of developing the script of the play was equal parts solitary work with the text and collaborative work with others. While many life history interviews that are transcribed and edited for an audience by ethnographers or oral historians are destined to stay as text, this work was always intended to become a script, and that required a hybrid process of writing and performance. It was almost impossible to know for certain how something I typed on the page would resonate in performance until I watched and listened to someone else read the work aloud.

By the winter of 2016, I had what I hoped was a full script, and an opportunity to present and test the work in a staged reading at UNC-Chapel Hill with Joseph Megel directing (see Figure 7). In the midst of rehearsals for that staging, I learned that I had received a grant to continue working on the project at UC San Diego, where I was by that time a postdoctoral researcher for the UC Collaboratory for Ethnographic Design. That grant allowed me to bring the script, revised once more after the staged reading, and translated back into Russian with the help of my Moscow colleague Valeriya Markina, back to my interlocutors in Russia for their input.

In the summer of 2016, my collaborator in Petrozavodsk Vladimir Rudak (on whose stories the Rudak character is based) helped me to set up a workshop with the people whose stories were represented in the script. Each person whose story was represented was invited to participate. Prior to circulating the script in full, each had the opportunity to review and suggest changes to the scene representing their own story (censoring elements they did not want publicly disclosed, pointing out inaccuracies, raising concerns about representation). At this point, one person chose to withdraw from the play, though not from the broader ethnographic project, preferring to not have a rather private story at the heart of the character portrait performed on stage (it would have been difficult to disguise this person's identity for a variety of reasons). Another person asked for me to remove a few comments about a family member. A few others raised concerns about the particular way that their speech was represented (e.g., the inclusion of filler words such as "like" or "um"), or the way that their character description depicted them. I of course acquiesced with the withdrawal, removing that monologue from the script. I also redacted the comments about the family member, and made a few other changes based on this initial remote feedback. I promised to bring up the other issues raised in the group discussion, as they concerned issues to do with the script as a whole. With these changes, I sent everyone a digital copy of the full, revised script for review about a week in advance of our in-person meeting.

On the day of our meeting (see Figure 5 and Figure 6), I brought a hardcopy of the script in Russian for each participant (and one in English – just for curiosity's sake, since only a few people would even admit to knowing any English). We proceeded to discuss the script in general, and problems of representation (of disability on stage, of Russia on stage, of personal stories in a public forum) and of authorship (one of the six participants declined to participate in the group meeting, and we had a separate one-on-one meeting). After some discussion, the group agreed that the script represented my own interpretation of their stories, and that with this in mind, it was useful to think of the script as a creative work. This allowed everyone to have input while avoiding the logistical and financial considerations required for a more elaborate process of consensus building and group authorship. It also offered an important caveat for some of the participants, in that they had the opportunity to claim plausible deniability: for example, to say that a given detail was an artistic embellishment that I had added. At least one participant was concerned about representation and anonymity, while others would have liked to be fully identified and claim their own stories. This required a degree of compromise. Another issue that came up was the style of language – some felt that given the opportunity they would like to revise the things that they had said two or more years before; others felt that it would be good to revise places where their wording was awkward. Some participants pointed out that awkwardness is what makes a script feel true-to-life. The group eventually agreed to put up with moments in which they felt the script made their character out to be inarticulate if it added dramatic purpose. I promised to take out extraneous filler language in one monologue, leaving only some "likes" and "ums" for dramatic effect.

We then proceeded to read through the script in full. Each scene was performed by someone other than the person whose story was represented in the scene; this was both funny, because it involved playing the role of someone who was sitting in the room, and allowed us to get the sense of the script as a play. By the end, everyone agreed that the most important thing was to make the play as entertaining as possible. The group came up with a variety of specific changes to make certain scenes funnier, or punchier, or more true to life, almost all of which have been incorporated into the final script. When it came to the question of representation, the group all agreed that it would be best to stage the play first in North America, then in Russian capital cities (Moscow, Saint Petersburg), and then only after theatrical success in these more fabled locales to stage a show regionally. They didn't want audiences at home to make the mistake of thinking that this play, like the Pushkin pageant, was just an amateur presentation intended for family members. Instead, this script, they hoped, would bring their stories to different audiences.

Following the group meeting, I met with as many of the participants as possible one-on-one. This gave everyone a chance to bring up issues they might not have wanted to discuss in front of the larger group or that came to them only upon reflection. I also visited and read through segments of the script with the participant who declined to attend the group meeting and asked for input on the major issues that we had discussed. I also met in person with the one participant who had withdrawn their consent to have their story adapted as part of the play; the participant explained the choice to withdraw in the context of life changes that had unfolded since we had last seen each other in person, while encouraging me to pursue the broader project.

Returning to the US, I revised the script based on the feedback from research participants. Already summer 2016, the next staging of the script was fast approaching in early fall: a staged workshop at UC San Diego. Director Joseph Megel and I had already spent a few weeks earlier in the summer conducting an initial round of casting and assembling a team of MFA students to design lights and sets.

With help from Julie Burelle, Yelena Gluzman, and others at UC San Diego, I scouted locations for workshop rehearsals and staging. And I spent hours poring over the details of the grant budget, crunching the numbers, and cross-checking my breakdown, often with financial officers in the Department of Communication.

From the earliest stages of planning the UC San Diego workshop I wanted to carry the collaboration with the research participants in the workshop process. With this in mind, I had set aside funds from a grant budget to bring two research participants to the workshop for two weeks. However, because most of the participants could not travel alone, in the end I had to settle for bringing one participant and a travel companion. Because Vladimir Rudak had his own creative projects that were ready to share in the US, it made sense for him to come to San Diego and take part in the staged workshop as a representative of the larger group (if we had had the funds, of course, it would have been better to bring everyone). Rudak composed an original score for the play: he created musical themes for each character. He performed these themes live on stage on acoustic guitar during the UC San Diego performances (see Figure 11). He also joined in at the end of the Rudak scene and took over the performance of the song from actor Jason Dorwart, who played the role of Rudak (see Figure 10). Throughout the rehearsal process, he participated in group rehearsals, consulting on questions about how to represent a particular moment, person, or place. Because Rudak doesn't understand much English, the questions were addressed to him in translation, either by me, by Olga Lazitski (a research assistant on the project who was then a graduate student in the Communication Department), or by Irina Dubova, the only one of the cast members who spoke Russian. After the workshop, he shared his observations about the process. Looking back, he was interested in the fact that the actors with disabilities in the workshop had professional training – something which he would like to see more of in Russia. Subsequently, Rudak's own play, based on his graphic novel, *I Am an Elephant*, has been staged in Saint Petersburg.

REPRESENTING RUSSIA ON THE NORTH AMERICAN STAGE

In the process of developing this play, my collaborators and I were aware that representing contemporary Russia on the North American stage presents a specific set of challenges. North Americans looking to inform the interpretation of a script about Russia draw on familiar representations of Russian characters and settings, but the representations of Russians in North American popular culture are limited. Actors and directors draw on their own experiences to make sense of a character's worlds and available sources to develop a vocabulary of embodied gestures and modes of speech. Likewise, set, costume, and lighting designers draw on their own cultural frameworks to interpret the words of the stage directions and scene descriptions to bring the world of the play to life on the stage. Performance is meaningful only by virtue of reference to a shared body of cultural symbols: audiences must interpret elements of a performance – from facial expressions to the quality of light cast on a set – based on knowledge they bring to the event. In turn, performance is itself expressive culture, and the meanings communicated through performance make up – and shift – cultural worlds (Fischer-Lichte 2014; Madison 2012). As I worked with director and performance ethnography practitioner Joseph Megel in the initial process of developing the script that became *I Was Never Alone*, we often worked to find shared points of reference that were at once true to my interlocutors' experience and resonant for North American audiences. For instance, while drafting scene and character descriptions, details that seemed significant to me were sometimes opaque or insignificant to Joseph and others who had not spent time in Russia. Some of those details remain in the finished script, with the idea that audiences with familiarity with Russia find them important, but balanced against other details that work more broadly. In those early playwriting workshop stages, reading pages aloud gave us space to flag those details that seemed culturally opaque; often I didn't get it right on the first try, but reworked scene and character descriptions based on feedback.

As a North American, I was aware that there are very few representations of daily life in contemporary Russia available for consumption. While the North American news media is rife with discussions of the machinations of Russian political and economic governance, the broader media landscape by and large leaves out the contours of work and play, home and family, and the arc of the life course for the general population of Russia. The few Hollywood films that depict Russia tend to be spy movies, with plots that turn on government coercion and extraordinary circumstances (e.g., *Red Sparrow* [2018]; *The Bourne Supremacy* [2004]). While these Hollywood depictions are distributed globally, very few Russian films make it into the popular consciousness of North American audiences, and those that do tend to reinforce existing stereotypes that circulate about Russia (for instance, the film *Leviathan* [2014]). These stereotypes understand Russia only as a bleak kleptocracy rife with corruption, misogyny, alcoholism, and violence, where only the very rich experience any kind of joy. Meanwhile, in contemporary Moscow, a film industry turns out a wealth of blockbusters, from action films to period pieces to romantic comedies, but these films almost never make it to North American audiences beyond the Russophone diaspora.[28] Very few Russians are mafiosos, spies, hackers, or political leaders and opposition protestors, but these are the Russians represented in anglophone media; miners, doctors, teachers, factory workers, corporate office workers, musicians, and hipster restaurateurs are left out.

The pervasive stereotypes that dominate contemporary North American discourse about Russia come largely from Cold War discourses that characterized Soviet people as unfeeling, downtrodden, and duped by their own economic system and government. As Alexei Yurchak (2006) has argued, Cold War logics in the West have persistently posited the US-Russia dichotomy as one in which Americans citizens are free, while Russians are deprived of liberty. Rather than conceptualizing shades of complexity, the predominant cultural viewpoint in the West insists on a stark divide between the free West and the repressed Soviet world (both of which persistently erase and draw their wealth from colonial encounters in the Global South). This cleavage of free/repressed extends to include a great number of characteristics: democratic/autocratic; honorable/corrupt; truthful/deceitful; joy/despair; real/fake; colorful/gray; wealthy/impoverished; just/unjust; objective/emotional; responsible/irresponsible; warm/cold (Yurchak 2006; Roudakova 2017). These representations proliferate across the pages of news reports. For instance, articles about the accusations that a Russian graduate student in the US was acting as foreign agent turn on the idea that Russians are duplicitous by nature and use evidence of Russianness – vodka drinking, manner of dress, accented English – as evidence of duplicity (e.g., Helderman et al. 2018). Hollywood representations of Russian characters by and large follow the same logic: sexy spies, greedy oligarchs, drunken men, and downtrodden grandmothers. Even where theater-makers and theater-goers are frequently familiar with pre-Soviet Russian classics (Chekov's *The Cherry Orchard* [1903], etc.), very little Russian theater from the Soviet period and from the contemporary period has been staged in North America.[29]

These stereotypes, combined with a pervasive lack of more nuanced representations of contemporary Russian life in popular media, formed the backdrop for the script development workshops and stagings for *I Was Never Alone*, informing our conversations about how to present nuanced and ethical representations of Russia on stage. As an anthropologist, I felt a responsibility to create a script that suggested stagings that, as much as possible, would not inadvertently reinforce these stereotypes. What does it mean to make a work for public consumption "about" a group of people? In practice, these concerns emerged in conversations about production design with creative teams for the script development workshops. Hearing about the script before reading it closely, I noticed that potential collaborators or audiences sometimes assumed that the work was set in a residential institution for people with disabilities, rather than in family apartments, an interpretation that to me seemed connected to popular depictions of Russia as a place where citizens are subordinated to institutions, or where human rights are violated. Another place where this concern emerged was in color palettes for production design. In one staged reading, we considered a lighting scheme that depicted cold, gray, winter light. I worried that using this lighting palette might inadvertently reinforce the notion that Russia is always cloaked in drab grays, an artifact of Cold War propaganda's lasting impact on the representations of the former Soviet Union in North American media.[30] While it is true that the region of Russia where the work is set does have long cold winters, in fact the quality of northern sunlight is not necessarily gray at all. Vibrant colors pervade daily life. Rivers and lakes reflect constantly shifting clouds over blue skies, and vibrant birch leaves that turn from incandescent yellow-green in spring to deep verdant green in summer and shocking

Figure 19 A popular image from the final years of the Soviet Union is the moment of the opening of the first McDonald's in 1990. The image, with its long line of Soviet citizens waiting for an American hamburger, neatly encapsulates the popular North American narrative that the Soviet people were literally starved for a taste of consumer life in capitalism and democracy. Historical interviews about the franchise's opening recall that personnel serving customers had to be trained specially to smile because, while a smile is a mark of good customer service in the US, Soviet transactions took place in an economy of scarcity with low motivation for stores or restaurants to sell more or compete with one another, and smiles were rarely used. (AP Photo/Alexander Zemlianichenko)[31]

yellow-orange in autumn. Businesses, shopping centers, clothing, billboards, and consumer goods in bright colors interrupt snowy landscapes with bursts of color. Warm apartment interiors are decorated with bright wallpaper, vibrant classical red woven rugs, and new furniture from IKEA. It is only the public-facing facades, entry halls, and stairwells of apartment buildings and publicly maintained buildings like schools and public offices that carry the legacy of communist low-budget communal property. Decolonizing the depictions of the former Soviet Union on stage requires an approach to production design that intentionally uses a full color palette. At the same time, resisting this "post-soviet" color palette presented another challenge: how could we imagine new ways to signify that action on stage is taking place "in Russia"?

In *I Was Never Alone* the lifeworlds of the characters exceed the contours of our familiar stereotypes. In contrast to the widely successful play *The Fairytale Lives of Russian Girls* (Miroshnik 2014), which cleverly engaged the stereotypes of Russian femininity (prostitutes, old hags, trophy wives) through a magical realist tour de force that disemboweled the stereotypes from within, in order to fill them in with more nuanced humanity, *I Was Never Alone*, crafted as it is from personal interviews with Russians with disabilities, does less explicit translation work as a script. Therefore, the responsibility to take on stereotypes falls on the cast, production team, and audience to encounter the textures of daily life in Russia as vibrant and agentive. As an ethnographer-playwright, at times I struggled with finding a balance in the script between what is said and left unsaid: the ethnographic impulse to record, interpret, and *tell* the reader what things mean (overtly performing the role of expert cultural translator) was a hard habit to break. Throughout the script development process, Joseph Megel reminded me that a playwright must trust the audience to participate in the interpretive work of understanding what is on stage, and trust the theater-makers to interpret what to put on stage. Rather than dictating elements of the performance through the script, we worked to develop a script wherein the dialogue itself would encourage critical consideration of representations of Russia.

Of course, the dialogue in the script, adapted from transcripts of interviews, is open to multiple interpretations, and there is an unevenness to the amount of cultural translation intended by the speaker in a given portrait or segment of dialogue. In some of the portraits, the characters' perception of how foreigners might view Russia comes through: Alina recognizes that Americans perceive themselves as more willing to engage in street protest and other acts of direct democracy than Russians; Sergei contrasts the way that Moscow and Hollywood depict heroism in popular films; Rudak uses an implicit assumption that the built environment in the West is more accessible than in Russia to drive home his points about the injustices that wheelchair users face. As actress Reagan Linton, who played Vera, observed, the challenge of the play for her was not representing disability but representing the emotional world of her character as a Russian woman. During rehearsals, significant attention and time were spent trying to workshop the emotional intention of Vera's wry commentary about her husband's gruff attitude or the day-in-day-out toil of housework. While Vera herself had delivered these observations in the interview as unemotional woman-to-woman jokes, the temptation for an American interpretation was to signal emotional distress.[32] In other cases, comments that may unwittingly serve to shore up North American stereotypes are delivered by characters oblivious to the way their remarks might be read by foreigners: Anya's closing comedic remarks about the slow grind of bureaucracy are meant as light humor, rather than dark despair; her aside that her father happened to be tipsy when she went to talk to him one afternoon on a public holiday is not meant to carry any more significance than to set the tone for the conversation, as if a North American made a similar comment about a conversation with a family member after a Labor Day barbecue. These culturally specific moments occur even in details as small as the gesture that Rudak should make when he exclaims the word "*mnye*" when describing his friend's saga to get a designated accessible parking space. In Russian, the word "*mnye*" means "to me," indicating that an external system is acting on an individual. In Russian the word should and can only be accompanied with a gesture toward the center of the speaker's chest, but North American actors speaking the line tend to throw their arms outward, in an exclamation of disbelief.

Translating humor across cultures is always difficult. North American performances of Russianness sometimes mistake Russophone irony as bitterness. In anglophone literature, irony is often understood to depict a tragic mismatch between the actual and literal meanings of an event. And so too ironic commentary in Russian is stylistically tied to the ways in which daily life goes awry. However, the Russian invocation of irony in casual conversation often indicates not only tragedy or bitter sarcasm but clever humor (for more on this dynamic, see Ries 1997). For instance, when Rudak relates his complaint about his friend's experience with accessible parking spaces he is intentionally entertaining his listener, promising an ironic and humorous end to an anecdote about an experience that everyone can relate to, *not* presenting a dire and depressing tale of woe. In fact, considering that Rudak's primary experience as a disability advocate comes from speaking with nondisabled Russians, his complaint about the

Figure 20 Joy, as an emotion and affective element of daily life, is rarely depicted in representations of Russia and the Soviet Union for anglophone audiences. This is a complicated scenario, in that there are indeed well-documented artworks from the Soviet Realist period of the Stalinist 1930s that are notorious for being relentlessly positive and joyful even when the realities of the situation in the Soviet Union during those years was one of dire economic distress, leaving communities underresourced and overworked. One popular song from that period, "Life Is Getting Happier," sums up the stylistic imperatives that Stalinist censors enforced during that era (von Geldern 1995). Yet, daily life in the Soviet Union and even in the difficult years of post-Soviet economic crisis still marched forward, and contemporary Russians who lived through the Brezhnev years of the 1960s and 1970s will often recall those years with fond nostalgia, a time when few in the Soviet Union wanted for material goods. These day-to-day moments of love, connection, and lightness were real, just as Americans in those eras experienced joy even in light of injustices committed at the hands of the US government, from McCarthyism to the Vietnam Draft. For example, this image depicts a young couple in love; the well-known film *Moscow Does Not Believe in Tears* (1980) depicts a midlife romance; Alexei Yurchak's interviewees in Leningrad/Saint Petersburg fondly recall creative jaunts in 1980s punk music and literary life (2006). (*Zdravstvui liubov'* [Hello love], Nina Sviridova and Dmitrii Vozdvizhenskii, c. 1960s–1970s, printed with permission of the estate)

bureaucratic ordeal entailed in negotiating over the parking space may be read as an assimilationist comment about how the life of a wheelchair user is just like the life of an ambulatory Muscovite. All the same, a North American listener who encounters the text without context might unwittingly hear this complaint as a morose meditation on insurmountable hurdles of life in a corrupt system.

The gap between North American and Russian cultural context is perhaps most apparent in the exchange between Alina and her mother about Russia's political history. Russians, like North Americans, are intimately familiar with the images, personality traits, and public personas of past political leaders. Like Reagan, or Eisenhower, or the elder Trudeau, to mention a past Russian political leader immediately calls up common popular narratives about the person and the role they played in the nation's history both as a figure of government and as a cultural icon. In this way, rehearsing the characteristics of past Soviet leaders as Alina and her mother do in their scene amounts to a playful volley that would be immediately accessible, familiar, and humorous to a listener at all familiar with Russian history. While it would be possible to play the scene as an actual argument or read it as a dire recitation of past wrongs, a more accurate interpretation is to stage it as light-hearted banter that both characters enjoy – Alina and Mama are showing off for their guest and having fun together.[33]

In still other moments in the play, the characters' narration unfolds without any regard for a North American audience's lack of familiarity with the Russian context. While this makes sense given the source material for the play, ethnographic interviews conducted in Russian in Russia with an anthropologist who is foreign but deeply enmeshed in local life, the absence of cultural translation in the characters' narratives may leave the reader, performer, or audience member without a reference point for how to interpret the cultural meaning and therefore the affective impact of particular details. For instance, Vera's commentary that her current husband is a veteran of the war in Chechnya leaves unmarked the fact that while the contours of that conflict were reported in North American news media at the geopolitical level, there is almost no sense in North American popular culture of the experience of the Russian soldier during and after this war, which unfolded throughout the early 2000s and facilitated Russia's anti-Muslim-extremist entry into the discursive global war on terror.

In another instance, Vakas references the game *Heaven* and goes on to describe a series of events that unfolded across his participation in Russophone online gaming culture with transmedia tie-ins – a cultural world unto itself. The decision to leave these details in the script was one that emerged through the collaborative experience of staging the play as a work-in-progress. In some cases, these details have niche audiences. For instance, the scene descriptions make references to ethnographic details that are at once obscure to some, and humorous in their familiarity to those who know contemporary Russia: at preliminary readings of the script, I noticed colleagues familiar with Russia chuckling at the mention of Ahmad Tea, Adidas sandals with socks worn as house slippers, and garish wallpaper. In these cases, I have tried to provide footnotes, and I urge those reading or performing the work to consult a collaborator familiar with contemporary Russian culture to make sense of these many diffuse, and culturally meaningful, details.

In this way, developing the script of *I Was Never Alone* has served as an experimental laboratory for observing North American perceptions of Russia, and as a collaborative project to decolonize representations of the affective life of the Russian citizen-subject. This involves the recognition that the post-Soviet mindset is not one that affects only the citizens of the region, but is rather a complex geopolitical and cultural worldview that is profoundly global (Fraser and Gordon 1994; Gille 2010; Suchland 2011). In developing this script with numerous collaborators, including research participants, theater artists, and audiences, I have sought to encourage the North American reader and performer to open themselves to the possibility that the affective lifeworlds of Russians are not as deeply alienated from a spectrum of emotion as popular depictions of authoritarianism would suggest. This possibility came most cogently to life through one unorthodox element of our San Diego staged workshop: in collaboration with director Joseph Megel, we elected to devote a significant portion of our workshop budget to bringing collaborator and research participant Vladimir Rudak to San Diego to participate in the workshop in person. This meant that throughout the rehearsal process questions and notes about how to play a particular line or character trait were as likely to be directed to Rudak as to me as the ethnographer-playwright. It also complicated the rehearsal process:

because Rudak speaks and understands little English, I often played the role of literal translator, quietly relating unfolding discussions to Rudak. While Rudak's role in the production was largely a creative one – he composed the original score for the performances – his behind the scenes presence foregrounded for everyone in the process the fact that the script was based on the adapted narratives of real people with multidimensional lives.

In his foundational treatise on the practice of ethnography, Bronislaw Malinowski laid out three kinds of observational action that the ethnographer should take, with the goal of discovering the "native" or insider's cultural point of view. Malinowski warns against the tendency to look at other cultural worlds solely through institutions and social norms; the ethnographer, he insists, must consider "the subjective desire of feeling" by which people live, tracking not only the technical differences between cultures, but attending to "the substance of their happiness" in order to approach a sense of understanding (Malinowski 1922; see also Narayan 2012, 14). Like Malinowski's maxim, if anglophone conversations on Russia continue to ignore happiness, desire, and joy in Russian social worlds, those conversations will miss the texture and substance of daily life. This does not mean that an anthropology ought to ignore suffering, injustice, and dynamics of power, but that representation without joy engenders pity and indifference rather than curiosity and respect.

SPOTLIGHT ON METHODS: Casting and Rehearsing Access
When we set out to cast the first public staged reading of *I Was Never Alone*, held in February 2016 at UNC-Chapel Hill, director and project collaborator Joseph Megel (artist-in-residence in performance studies there) and I sought to cast actors with disabilities in as many roles as possible, because the staging would be a process reading intended to develop the play, and because we were working with a very modest budget cobbled together from various units around campus. After a few moonshot attempts to increase the budget came up short, we settled on casting student actors

and community actors who were interested in the exposure, willing to rehearse for a week, and to perform with no compensation besides transportation costs and a few meals. Joseph had long been doing work in social justice-oriented theater, including performance ethnography projects (such as directing a Durham staging of E. Patrick Johnson's *Sweet Tea*), many of which he supported through various stages of development in a long-running process series. While I was leaning on his experience casting similar projects in Chapel Hill, he was new to working on shows with disability as a major theme. We decided to draw on Joseph's background casting "against race" as a justice-oriented measure to improve acting possibilities for artists of color to our casting practices for disability theater. I knew already that the practice of casting nondisabled actors in main roles in plays and films about disability experience was widely disdained in the disability justice blogosphere and in academic disability studies. When colleagues put me in touch with other playwrights working on plays with disabilities outside of dedicated disability theater companies they supported the working approach that Joseph and I had come up with, confirming that others were using similar techniques. So our approach was this: we would set out to cast actors with disabilities as much as possible but our objective would be to cast disabled actors in the play, not to "match" a given character's diagnosis with the specific disability that an actor identified with.

By the fall of 2015, I was already in San Diego working as a postdoctoral researcher for the UC Collaboratory for Ethnographic Design. I took a trip back to North Carolina in mid-fall to work on plans for the play. We designed a casting call and held an initial round of auditions. While this seemed audaciously far in advance to be casting for such a short process, I was worried that in a regional scene like Chapel Hill we would need time to find actors. Indeed, the casting process occupied a great deal of time, and the logistics of transporting actors with mobility impairments – often on the way home from the theater late in the evening after rehearsals and performances – was an additional production element that for that first reading I absorbed into my own workload as playwright-ethnographer ... and producer/production assistant (managing the budget and fundraising) ... and access coordinator for both backstage and front-of-house issues.

By the time we got around to planning the San Diego staged workshop, I was sure that I wanted to expand the engagement with questions of disability access. We already knew that the script, in principle, worked as a play. But after conversations with playwright Deborah Stein at UC San Diego, I was eager to understand what specifically this work might do theatrically, given how heavily the interview-based script relied on text. I felt that a deeper engagement with the moral and ethical questions of disability access might bring about new aesthetic possibilities.

Thanks to a generous grant for a transdisciplinary performance ethnography project I was able to hire Louise Hickman, then a PhD candidate in the Communication Department at UC San Diego researching critical disability studies, accessibility, and care. I asked Louise to come onto the project not only as a sort of coordinator but as an accessibility researcher. I suggested that she might use the staged workshop as a kind of lab to explore problems and issues in accessibility that were of relevance to her own research (Hickman completed her dissertation on the access work involved in simultaneous real-time transcription work in 2018). Indeed, this is what she did. After doing some reading on various techniques for making theater more accessible for people with sensory impairments, Hickman observed that many mainstream modes of thinking about disability access understood it as something to be added after the fact, without any significant or noticeable aesthetic effect on the performance or theater-creation process. She suggested that we experiment with what might happen if we worked access in from the beginning, as part of the process, and as part of the aesthetic of the show.

In order to do this, Hickman made several innovations. First, she urged director Joseph Megel to consider what might happen if scene description for people with visual impairment were somehow integrated into the performance itself. Megel agreed that particularly in a staged reading it was possible to use a reader's theater idiom, wherein actors not in a given scene act as narrators, reading the excerpts from the scene description in a script to introduce the scene. In the talkback session after the show, Megel reflected that in conversations with Hickman, she pushed him to think differently about who the intended audience for the work might be and about how theatrical performance is perceived by audience members.

Second, Hickman was curious to expand on other sensory access elements. American Sign Language (ASL) interpreting and simultaneous transcription are typical access options for audience members with hearing impairments (we staggered these two methods between performances). But, Hickman pointed out that for people with both vision and hearing impairment ASL is difficult to see, and while simultaneous transcription (wireless transmitted to one's own device) is easier to see, in order to read along one has to also look down, thereby missing action that is taking place on stage. Traditionally, stenographers are trained as neutral observers and only transcribe what they hear onstage. But this means that a transcriptionist leaves out any information that does not come in the form of speech: nonspoken parts, such as facial expressions, are not rendered in standard transcription. Moreover, there is a short delay of several seconds between a word being spoken and the word appearing in the transcription. This means that the audience member following the transcription will experience the performance on a different temporal beat from the audience following the action on stage directly. For instance, when Vera makes a joke about cleaning up the kitchen after her husband when he "helpfully" cooks dinner, the audience member following the transcription may hear other audience members around them laugh four or five seconds before the punchline appears in the transcription. And, when an actor delivers a line with the kind of expert comedic timing that elicits a guffaw or laugh at the audacity of the character's point of view – for instance in Jason Dorwart's rendition of Rudak's discussion of living "in the frozen north" – the audience member following a standard transcription is not privy to the communicative nuance of the line's delivery that elevates it from blithe sarcasm to scathing laugh line. Finally, there are moments in the theatrical performance when nonverbal communication carries a great deal of meaning, but much of these gestures and facial expressions are filled in by actors and directors and never appear in the script or in written transcriptions of the words the actors speak – and here, again, the standard transcription is not designed to convey this information. To address this design gap Hickman came up with a creative innovation: she invited artist and story-teller Kate Clark to participate in the project as a scene describer. She seated the storyteller next to the stenographer so they can work together to transcribe verbal and nonverbal forms of communication as they occur onstage.

At the start of the performance, during the curtain speech, Hickman and I welcomed audience members to the theater and explained that unlike in other theater performances that they may have attended at this performance the elements of accessibility would not be hidden but would be part of the aesthetic of the event. Hickman, taking a feminist science and technology studies (STS) approach to theorizing access, is interested in making visible the elements of networks that constitute access-providing systems. This ethos of exposing or making visible the labor of access work is central to Hickman's work as a scholar-activist. Where usually at the curtain speech audience members are reminded to turn off their cell phones, here we asserted that audience members were encouraged to leave their cell phones on and to be aware that other audience members may be using their screens for accessibility purposes. We urged audience members who might hear the storyteller's comments to a transcriptionist to think of this auditory information not as a distraction but part of the aesthetic of access that the process hoped to develop. Those who felt that they would be distracted by this sound were encouraged to move to another seat. Some audience members seemed befuddled by this question, and certainly the experimental vibe may have been off-putting to some. We also pointed out that if audience members were interested in the original Russian, they could follow along with the Russian-language script via a webpage listed in the program (which also included a reprint in both Russian and English of the poem from Vakas's scene and the lyrics to the song performed by Rudak).

Disability theater is persistently addressed with a simple and important question: "What should accessibility mean in theatre?" (Johnston 2012, 160). The array of responses to the question of access at the theater and in theater-making has not been resolved but has been approached quite differently by a variety of different practitioners. On the one hand, mainstream, high-end theater tends to think of access in terms of special provisions added on to a theatrical performance to facilitate the attendance of audience members with disabilities. For instance, new autism-friendly performances of Broadway musicals designate specific shows to accommodate autistic theater-goers and their families. Or specific shows are designated as ASL-interpreted. Audio description may be provided via headsets so that vision-impaired theater-goers can listen to descriptions without disturbing the experience of nondisabled audience members seated around them (Johnston 2012). This approach is quite different from more avant-garde productions that seek to reconfigure the aesthetics of theater-making in terms of integrating a crip politics at every level of theatrical process (e.g., Sins Invalid 2015). Audience access aside, access to professional theater training, roles, and funding for production for and by disabled artists is another problem: barriers facing various groups in the broader disability community are uneven, with racialized and poor folks facing more barriers than white folks and little access for people with intellectual disabilities to artmaking outside of therapeutic or pedantic contexts.

I Was Never Alone's process has engaged the space of theatrical production as a space for research. In the performance ethnography tradition, the work of making a piece of theater is a space for experimentation and observation. Future performances of the play will work out different schemas for extending disability access in new ways, and centering disability expertise in the process. But, access is not a checklist or an endpoint that we can arrive at – rather it is a messy social process of care and negotiating social and material relationships.

CONCLUSION

In *I Was Never Alone*, the main characters, *oporniki*, hold together community and kin by engendering intimacy through demands for care made palpable by relational performances of disability. Many representations of people with disabilities in the ethnographic records get stuck in the task of describing how a given person came to occupy a role of social abjection, entrenched in and reentrenching what Joel Robbins (2013, following Trouillot 2003) describes as postcolonial anthropology's fixation on the suffering subject. Even though medical anthropology has long criticized the ways in which medicalization individualizes pathology, the category of disability in anthropological treatments has often focused on how individual diagnoses come into being or are taken up globally, thereby leaving the category of disability itself uninterrogated.

Disability anthropology that engages with the critiques levied by disability studies, not only of the medical model of disability but of the narrative prothesis by which disability comes to carry and hold particular symbolic social meanings, is now in a new era of florescence. It is to this conversation that I enter *I Was Never Alone*, not only as a performative work, but as a methodological specimen that cracks open some of the concerns that the disability critique brings to the ethnographic project.

By imagining *oporniki* not as in need of cure or somehow deficient, we open the possibility to understand the "never aloneness" of the narrators as fostering relationships of care that create novel configurations of emotive affinity. Rather than imagining disability as a marker of those who require care as vulnerable in the sense of suffering and deserving of pity, we can understand disability as a performative relation of vulnerability that has a unique capacity to foster social bonds. Thinking of disability in this way, we might imagine each of the scenes in *I Was Never Alone* as representing the backbone of a network of kinship and care. The minor characters who enter scenes (physically or by phone calls) and the audience (performing the role of ethnographer/ listener) become a part of the choreographed network of social worlds that each character holds together. In theorizing disability through this performance ethnography project, I find myself reframing *the need for care* or *request for accommodation* as a unique structural capacity to produce performances of kinship, intimacy, and belonging. If performance requires us to recognize the ways that we are becoming together, and a queer feminist politics of interdependency requires us to recognize nonnormative relationships of care as the backbone of the social organism, then none of us, truly, were ever alone.

There are myriad ways of creating extraordinary circumstances for collaborative knowledge production; performance is but one of them.[34] It is this labor that offers the transformative potential of performance. By committing to a performance paradigm, the ethnographer commits to collaborative knowledge production, and being together in space and time, not only with research participants, but also with performers, designers, and audiences. This is a design for knowledge production that demands that the ethnographer work in many cases as a producer – calling into being the social configurations that make up performance: table readings, script edits, feedback, design team meetings, auditions and casting meetings, and so forth. To commit to the performance paradigm means mobilizing the creative labor of a great many others besides the ethnographer and the research participants. In this way, performance ethnography lays bare one nagging concern of the ethnographic project: the question of whether participating in the research really delivers value (aside from the value to the ethnographer's own career). The ethnographer now must not only build rapport and reciprocity or offer compensation to interviewees, but must also broker sustainable relationships (through compensation for labor, satisfying collaboration, or some combination thereof) with artistic collaborators. This makes the work of ethnographic theater costly – both financially and emotionally – for the ethnographer, even assuming the requisite expertise. And, to the extent that the ethnographer-playwright participates in the scene of theatrical creation, the theater where the ethnographic play is staged becomes a space of participant observation. Moreover, the creative collaborators in the theatrical space also must perform "the labor of being studied" (Cowan and Rault 2014): when their interpretive labor in rehearsals and performances becomes the object of the ethnographer-playwright investigation, they are in effect asked to perform an additional role, that of research subject.

Performance ethnography will not save us. It will not stop suffering. It will not prevent researchers from taking advantage of privileges to skew power relations with coperformers-interlocutors to benefit the researcher rather than the community. Encountering performance works may or may not move audiences and theater-makers to change. What performance ethnography *does* do is expose ethnographers to a different nodal network of bringing a project to its apex, and in so doing it exposes kinds of knowledge, labor, and taken-for-granted assumptions that writing alone leaves unexamined.

The observations put forth in these notes are necessarily inchoate. The life of this play, like the life of any work of ethnographic writing, will move on beyond my own capacity to shape its interpretation and impact. As a work of performance, the play script itself calls for aesthetic, embodied, three-dimensional interpretations, to be repeated many times, never once exactly alike. Interpretations will be manifold and layered one atop another: reader, director, dramaturg, actor, audience, retellings about "the play I saw last weekend." My own research on this topic has hardly ended, but rather is just beginning. As the script moves and breathes in its own way, my fieldsite as ethnographer expands; in coming years, new productions will offer new backstage scenes to record and ponder. Just as my life has moved on in many ways since I first began this research six years ago, so too have the lives of my interlocutors. Their own creative projects have blossomed and been presented, life stages shifted, vulnerabilities negotiated. The performance of the ethnographic ritual does not end with representation, the publication of a manuscript, or presentation of a play: the vulnerability of the return rears on the horizon, the sense of something shared now past like a brush of sensation, the memory of something fleeting that transpired once, a sliver of being together in time that we attempted to capture, freeze, create anew. Ritual vulnerability produces a sense of "we" whose meanings refuse to hold fixed.

NOTES

1 Where performance ethnography has circulated in performance studies and theater studies beyond anthropology departments, as an anthropologist trained in both cultural anthropology and performance ethnography methods, with this project I seek to bring the transformed ethnography back to my home discipline.

2 Some examples of disability anthropology as I define it here include
   Friedner (2015); Wool (2015); Kulick and Rydstrom (2015); Nakamura
   (2013); Landsman (2009); Biehl and Eskarod (2005); and Frank (2000).

3 Many scholars of disability studies have observed that just as gender is a
   social formation that has meaning only in relation to other categories of
   social difference – race, class, colonial position, ethnicity, sexuality, and
   so on – so too, disability makes sense as an identity around which to organize liberatory movements only in relation to other systems of oppression. In particular, race, ethnicity, colonization, access to health care, and
   civil rights claims all produce different experiences of disability.

4 I would very much like to see a survey of cultural works created by
   people with disabilities in Russia; to my knowledge such a volume does
   not currently exist in either Russian or in English. As Russian disability
   studies continues to grow, new works are being published that take up
   these projects, increasingly in English. While there are a great many film-
   makers, artists, performers, and so on with disabilities working in Russia
   whose work I follow, I do not have space to discuss these works or their
   creators herein. As an ethnographer, I am also interested in tracking representations of disability in contemporary popular media, though usually as a mode of contextualizing ethnographic research (e.g., Hartblay
   2014, 2019).

5 Often, disability studies and disability anthropology have divided the
   world into North and South, allowing these geographic territories to
   gloss the difference between colonizing and colonized, developed and
   developing societies (e.g., Ingstad and Whyte 1995, 2007; Friedner and
   Zoanni 2018). When it comes to the former Soviet Union, the question
   of a North/South divide presents a problem (Iarskaia-Smirnova 2001).
   Usually, in academic and popular discourse the problems of development are understood to exist in the so-called Global South, or postcolonial world (as opposed to the settler colonies of North American and
   the colonizing global center of Northern Europe). Yet, as others have
   argued, this leaves out the region of the world that this study considers
   (Wiedlack and Neufeld 2016; Suchland 2011). Thus, disability identity in
   Russia should be understood not only in terms of the institutions of the
   nation-state but also in terms of the development and democratization
   projects that foreign entities enacted in the immediate post-Soviet years,
   typically glossed as the transition from state socialism to democracy and
   global capitalism. In my broader research on disability in Russia, I have

found that historical Soviet ideas about what counts as a normal body and about what citizens can expect from the state continue to shape how people with disabilities make claims for their own interest and well-being today. We might think of this formulation as a detransitional view of post-Soviet Russia.

6 See Appendix 3 for a timeline of political leaders of Russia.

7 The program of democratization in Russia in the immediate post-Soviet period of the 1990s was deeply reliant on a Cold War discourse that understood global economies in terms of a unilineal track of economic development. This development posited an undivorceable relationship between democratic governance and capitalism, in which each required the other to thrive (a supposition which even Francis Fukuyama, who (in)famously proclaimed the end of the USSR the end of history, has now admitted is deeply flawed [1989, 2012], as both Russia and the United States veer toward a new era of authoritarian capitalism). Anastasia Kayiatos (2013) has posited a unique relationship between the American Cold War vision of post–Soviet Russia as "slow to develop" market economics and civil society, and deeply emotionally limited, as predicated on a profoundly ableist concept of development. In this collapsing of metaphors, the nation state is personified, and also racialized through a pathologization of behavioral capacities. Similarly, I have described a version of this logic in action in the American villainization of Vladimir Putin, which I dub *disorderization* (Hartblay 2015).

8 The nuances of Alina's response to her mother's comment is discussed further in Jason Dorwart's 2016 article about the play in *TheatreForum*.

9 There are many different ways that the concept of disability can be phrased in English and in Russian; each carries a variety of associations for different groups of people. In this book, I use the phrases "people with disabilities" and "disabled people" interchangeably. This reflects the particular moment of writing (when there is a divide in the English-speaking disability community over which of these phrases is most empowering – "people first language" that phrases disability as something that one possesses but which need not define or overdetermine a person's identity, or, "social model" language that thinks of disabled as an adjective that need not be negative, and of the way that people with impairments are "disabled by society," locating disability not in a body, but in social relations). Of course, in the context of this play, the issue is further complicated by the variegation of words and phrases

for disability in Russian. For more on this topic, see Appendix 2, as well as the history chapter of Sarah Phillip's (2011) book on disability in Ukraine.

10 People with disabilities are represented as marginalized frequently in ethnographic monographs, for example, the residents of Vita in Joao Biehl and Torben Eskorod's (2005) ethnography of a "zone of social abandonment." Meanwhile, Kulick and Rydstrom's (1998) volume *Loneliness and Its Opposite* explicitly examines the relationship of significant disability to loneliness, or sets out to do so according to its title.

11 The practice of capitalizing "Deaf" to identify a cultural group is one that Friedner identifies as difficult to translate across cultural contexts. Here, I have used a lowercase letter, following Friedner's usage (2015, 12–14).

12 I use the phrase "compulsory able-bodiedness" following Alison Kafer's (2003) elaboration of Robert McRuer's (2002) riff on Adrienne Rich's (1980) phrase "compulsory heterosexuality." And, furthermore, in thinking about a critical global disability ethnography raises the question: What are the varied cultural formations of compulsory able-bodiedness that we might track across human societies?

13 That is, the category of disability that this play represents is one that is based on local histories of a shifting landscape of education and social services that, based on a medical model, considered motor and neurological disorders as a category of disablement, and the community that developed out of those social contexts. Meanwhile, the research city was home to disability communities related to other locally meaningful categories including deafness, blindness, intellectual disabilities, and so forth.

14 The renowned nineteenth-century Russian author and playwright Anton Chekov is widely quoted as arguing for an economy of theatrical elements, with the idea that if an element that does not have bearing on a plot is introduced on stage, audience members will notice it and sit waiting for something that never comes. This precept is often referred to using the example of a pistol that appears on stage but is never fired (indeed, Chekov is quoted as having used this example, see Rayfield [2000]). By extension, we could imagine that Chekov would argue that good playwriting ought not to include a character with a limp or some other disability if the disability does not play a role in the plot.

15 Anthropologists understand *ritual* as a socially performed *rite* that signifies passage from one social state to another. A rite, in this sense, is a kind

of formalized or prescribed social action (that often takes the form of a performance). Rituals in the anthropological sense herald a transformation in social status (Turner 1995, developing Van Gennep's [1960] notion of rites of passage). For instance, common rituals in North American society include wedding ceremonies, graduation ceremonies, citizenship ceremonies, bar and bat mitzvahs, and so forth. In each of the ceremonies, participants appeal to a higher authority – secular or religious – to bestow a change in status (two people become married through the power of the state or of a religious power; students become graduates and bearers of a degree bestowed by the educational institution; residents become legal citizens of a nation state; children become men and women as dictated by the higher power of the Jewish faith). Anthropologists have traditionally investigated ritual ceremonies across cultures as an important way to learn about social status and shared cultural symbols in a given cultural group. However, the practice of ethnographic fieldwork is a ritual in itself: the ethnographer moves from being an outsider who does not know the ways and shared cultural knowledge of insiders; to conducting the rite known as "fieldwork"; to reporting back to another social group on the cultural knowledge gleaned through fieldwork, and thus becoming an "ethnographer of" some particular group or phenomenon. Here, the higher power can only be understood as the epistemological system that underlies the history of anthropological thought (see, for example, Murphy 2016), a powerful secular authority. Theater, too, requires a series of ritualized actions – entering a theater, watching and listening to or otherwise sensing a performance, leaving and discussing the meaning of that performance. In this case, the higher power reference is perhaps more complex to name, though a sort of secular civic sense of shared purpose might be identified.

16 Madison (2012) also distinguishes between performance ethnography and *performed ethnography*, the dialogic and collaborative interpretive process that ensues from the theatrical performance of ethnographic research.

17 Conquergood (2002) argues that academic writing has the effect of reinscribing the hegemony of text as a vehicle for the production and distribution of knowledge. He argues that this *textocentrism* has historically been complicit in colonial projects, and proposes collaborative, community-based performance ethnography as a possible way out of the academic adherence to textocentrism. Of course, performance and

theatre cannot be understood as wholly outside of colonizing processes, but should also be analyzed for possible complicity including cultural imperialism and cultural appropriation. Furthermore, writing authority into a text is also a kind of performance (Pollock 1998).

18 Of course, there is a rich history of theorizing the life of texts and the myriad ways in which texts are interpreted and performed, from Bakhtin to Derrida. A play script, too, is a kind of text, and the composition of a play script is a kind of writing practice. Yet the way that we enact text through theatrical performance – the visceral, interpretive work of acting and the collaborative work of staging – is a unique set of practices that shift social relations in specific ways.

19 Of course, there are other examples of anthropological engagements with theatre, some of which have been remembered, and others of which have been largely forgotten. For example, in his biography of anthropologist of Africa Colin Turnbull, Roy Richard Grinker details Turnbull's rather significant engagement with theatrical adaptations, and hints at its potential impact on 1970s US anthropology. British theater director Peter Brook and his experimental theater group, the International Centre of Theatre Research in Paris (known for the film version of the *Lord of the Flies*), adapted and directed anthropologist Colin Turnbull's controversial ethnography *The Mountain People* into a play, titled *The Ik* (*Les Iks*) (Grinker 2000, 210). Brook (2000, 211–15) took on the project after taking a troupe of European actors on a tour through Africa, seeking to understand something about the essential nature of performance. Deciding to seek a story related to Africa, but somewhat removed from the direct experience of the tour, Brook worked with stage and screen writers and with Turnbull himself to adapt the book into a play, ultimately settling on a method of improvisation with a group of international actors to devise an interpretation of Turnbull's ethnography. Interestingly, according to Richard Roy Grinker's study of the subject, the group reviewed images and film footage of *The Ik* taken during Turnbull's research period but did not review images or footage of Turnbull himself, though the anthropologist was a central character in the play. Turnbull (2000, 216–19) himself reflected later, and during discussions surrounding the American tour of the play at major university campuses, on the way that viewing the work changed him, and in particular, that he was distressed by the selfish foolishness of the young European depicted on stage. Turnbull "pondered aloud the question of whether theater and theatrical

workshops might help students learn that drama can often educate the public about culture more effectively than a 'discursive,' 'written' communication" reports Grinker (2000, 234–5), suggesting that Turnbull's involvement with theater preceded later shifts in anthropological critiques of logocentrism in the 1980s. After touring the US with the theatrical workshop, Grinker (2000, 235) writes that Turnbull said of anthropological fieldwork: "If you want to convey something of the quality of life in that society or of social forces like love and religious faith at work, then you can't do that by objective study. Your participation has to be internal. When Jerzy Grotowski [Polish avant-garde theater director] talks about acting, he says the actor should be aware of the possibility of becoming someone other than himself. When this happens it is the greatest moment in an actor's life; he makes a total sacrifice of self. For the anthropological, too!" Victor Turner (1982, 91) subsequently cited the collaboration between Turnbull and Brook as the proof of concept that "persuaded" him "that cooperation between anthropological and theatrical people was not only possible but also could become a major teaching tool for both sets of partners."

20 Norman K. Denzin (2003, 4) writes, helpfully summarizing several generations of thought: "The ethnographer moves from a view of performance as imitation, or dramaturgical staging (Goffman 1959), to an emphasis on performance as liminality and construction (Turner 1986a), then to a view of performance as struggle, as intervention, as breaking and remaking, as kinesis, as a sociopolitical act (Conquergood 1998, 32)."

21 For similar recent examples, see Cavanagh (2013); *Sweet Tea: Black Gay Men of the South*, written and performed by E. Patrick Johnson and directed by Joseph Megel. I saw a performance at the Durham Arts Council, Durham, NC in 2014, and the work is also published as a script (Johnson 2020).

22 I am reminded of a James Baldwin quote that I came across recently: "When you're writing, you're trying to find out something which you don't know" (Baldwin 1984, quoted in Temple 2018).

23 The full script includes a Russian-language option for this exchange, which actors and directors may choose to employ. For simplicity, here I have only included the English.

24 These crip kinship relations do not have terms in standard Russian. In the play, Anya refers to her as a housemate, *sosedka* in Russian, the standard term for neighbor or housemate who is not a blood relation, but distinct from *sidelka* or other words designating a uni-directional

relationship of care, like attendant, sitter, or housekeeper. Like the creative kinds of crip kinship described by Piepnez-Samarasinha, the undistinguished words for the relationships are insufficient markers for the important work that these care webs do.

25   While Reagan's comment about acting stands, disability theatre, even when the subject matter is not disability per se, is deeply entwined with disability politics. That is, the politics of exclusion and access enter into the staging of any show in which disabled actors perform. Can disabled actors get on the stage (Johnston 2012, 3; Kuppers 2017, 5)? Will the audience always be primarily nondisabled people? As disability arts curator Sean Lee has put it, when disability arts are always led by nondisabled makers and cater to nondisabled audiences, it means always starting again from square one. The expertise developed through generations of disability culture, passing on techniques and knowledge, cannot be taken for granted, but must be built from the ground up. It means learning the same lesson over and over again. As Simi Linton (1998, 117) wrote in her seminal text, "'Disability studies' ... organizes and circumscribes a knowledge base that explains the social and political nature of the ascribed category, disability." The ethos of disability culture argues that inaccess for one person is unacceptable, and the aesthetic practices that shape every phase of the theatrical process are foundationally grounded in rituals of vulnerability and the commitment to crip time that is required to facilitate radical access. With this in mind, as this manuscript goes to press, I am currently in the process of planning a disability arts, disability-maker-led production of *I Was Never Alone* in Toronto.

26   At the time, I worked at CEC ArtsLink, on a program hosting award-winning young artists from Russia for residences in the US. In this case the playwrights had a residency at Princeton University hosted by Sergeui Oushakine, and our organization hosted a staged reading of excerpts from their work at the Living Theatre in New York.

27   In the summer of 2019, after over a decade of acting as the driving force behind Teatr.doc, the early and unexpected death of Elena Gremina was announced, only a few short months after the death of her husband and the cofounder of Teatr.doc. Following on not long after what was widely understood to be a political arrest of theater director Kirill Serebrennikov, Gremina's death prompted speculation that Teatr.doc was perceived by Russian authorities to be politically dangerous. Meanwhile, Serebrennikov was on trial in Moscow for alleged corruption on what

his colleagues widely asserted were politicized and trumped up charges (BBC 2018; Janney 2017; Freedman 2017).

28 US Amazon Prime video streaming does hold many of these titles in its catalog, with subtitles, but due to algorithms aimed at existing preferences, few viewers beyond the Russophone diaspora will find them.

29 A press release about the staged reading of works of New Russian theater in New York included the following:

> Even the most devoted of New York theater-goers would be hard-pressed to name a Russian playwright other than Anton Chekov. Sergeui Oushakine, Professor of Slavic Languages and Literatures at Princeton, and the playwright's host during their time there, highlights this gap:
>
> > Theatre and Drama are generally underrepresented in the Slavic curriculum in the United States. We know the poetry and the fiction that has come out of Russia in the past fifty years, but, partly because dramatic work has largely gone untranslated, Slavic scholars are familiar with Chekov and other 19th century playwrights, but with nothing contemporary. Which is really a shame because theater is such a booming cultural field in Russia today. So hopefully with this exchange we will start to fill in that gap.
>
> Although there has been a growing turn toward contemporary theatre in US Slavic Languages and Literatures programs (see, for example, the work of Lipovetsky, Weygandt, and others), as Oushakine went on to underline in this quote for the press release, the general public has still had very little contact with contemporary Russian theater. If anything, the state of cultural exchange has declined since 2009.

30 I am not the first to note the relationship between color palette and emotive range in depictions of Russia and postsocialism. For instance, Fehérváry (2013) describes the perception of color in capitalist consumer life opposed to the greyness of socialist apartment blocks. Alaina Lemon (2008) writes:

> Anglophone historians work to revise the vision of sentiment in late Soviet society (for examples, see Siegelbaum 2006; Field 2007) – but their representations are not the ones that disseminate the farthest. Hollywood cinema, time and again, painted the two worlds with a separate color pallete for each side of the Iron Curtain: returning to the West was a return to

the world of colors. Colors signified expression, "freedom" from totalitarian planning, openness to contingency and emotion. (245)

31 For a brief and accessible discussion of the opening of McDonald's in the Soviet Union, see the episode "The New Norm" from the podcast *Invisibilia*, https://www.npr.org/programs/invisibilia/481887848 /the-new-norm?showDate=2016-06-17.

32 Another element of Reagan's work to interpret Vera is the very different tone of US and Russian feminisms.

33 In contrast, when the two scenes of the play were performed in Russian in a reading at European University in the fall of 2018 the actors themselves selected the Alina scene, saying that given its familiarity and ubiquitous themes it offered an easy point of entry for an audience, and therefore an opportunity for the performers to draw out the humor in the cheerful familial banter.

34 However, there is something particular about the relationship between disability or "extraordinary bodies" in Rosemarie Garland-Thomson's (1997) phrase, and the potentiality for performances that offer "extraordinary movement," as contemporary dance curator Emma Gladstone has termed it (British Council Arts n.d.).

REFERENCES

Addlakha, Renu. 2020. "Kinship Destabilized! Disability and the Micropolitics of Care in Urban India." *Current Anthropology* 61 (S21): S46–54. https://doi.org/10.1086/705390

Baldwin, James. 1984. Interviewed by Jordan Elgrably. 1984. "The Art of Fiction No. 78." https://www.theparisreview.org/interviews/2994 /james-baldwin-the-art-of-fiction-no-78-james-baldwin.

Barnes, Colin, and Geoff Mercer. 2001. "Disability Culture: Assimilation or Inclusion?" In *Handbook of Disability Studies*, 515–34. Thousand Oaks, CA: Sage Publications.

Bauman, H. Dirksen L., and Joseph J. Murray. 2010. "Deaf Studies in the 21st Century: 'Deaf-Gain' and the Future of Diversity." In *The Oxford Handbook of Deaf Studies, Language, and Education*, edited by Marc Marschark and Patricia Elizabeth Spencer, 210–25. Vol. 2. New York: Oxford University Press.

–, eds. 2014. *Deaf Gain: Raising the Stakes for Human Diversity*. Minneapolis: University of Minnesota Press.

BBC. 2018. "Russian Director Goes on Trial for Fraud," 7 November. https:// www.bbc.com/news/world-europe-46125108.

Bell, Chris. 2010. "Is Disability Studies Actually White Disability Studies?" In *The Disability Studies Reader*, 3rd ed., edited by Lennard J. Davis, 374–82. London: Routledge.

Beumers, Birgit, and M.N. Lipovetsky. 2009. *Performing Violence: Literary and Theatrical Experiments of New Russian Drama*. Bristol, UK: Intellect.

Biehl, João, and Torben Eskerod. 2013. *Vita: Life in a Zone of Social Abandonment*. Updated with a New Afterword and Photo Essay edition. Berkeley: University of California Press.

Brannon, Ruth. 1995. "The Use of the Concept of Disability Culture: A Historian's View." *Disability Studies Quarterly* 15 (4): 3–15.

British Council Arts. n.d. Disabled Leaders in Dance. YouTube. Accessed 31 January 2016, https://www.youtube.com/watch?v=2A7AjmfpNY4.

Brown, Steven. 2002. "What Is Disability Culture?" *Disability Studies Quarterly* 22 (2). https://doi.org/10.18061/dsq.v22i2.343.

Carlson, Marvin. 2003. *The Haunted Stage: The Theatre as Memory Machine*. Ann Arbor: University of Michigan Press.

Cavanagh, Sheila L. 2013. "Affect, Performance, and Ethnographic Methods in Queer Bathroom Monologues." *Text & Performance Quarterly* 33 (4): 286–307. https://doi.org/10.1080/10462937.2013.823513.

Chekhov, Anton Pavlovich. 1991. *The Cherry Orchard*. Dover Thrift Editions. New York: Dover Publications.

Clare, Eli. 2015. *Exile and Pride: Disability, Queerness, and Liberation*. Durham, NC: Duke University Press.

Clifford, James, and George Marcus, eds. 2010. *Writing Culture: The Poetics and Politics of Ethnography*. 25th anniversary ed. Berkeley: University of California Press.

Cohen, Lawrence. 1998. *No Aging in India: Alzheimer's, the Bad Family, and Other Modern Things*. Berkeley: University of California Press.

Conquergood, Dwight. 1988. "Health Theatre in a Hmong Refugee Camp: Performance, Communication, and Culture." *TDR: The Drama Review* 32 (3): 174–208.

– 2002. "Performance Studies: Interventions and Radical Research." *TDR: The Drama Review* 46 (2): 145–57.

– 2006. "Rethinking Ethnography: Towards a Critical Cultural Politics." In *The Sage Handbook of Performance Studies*, edited by D. Madison and Judith Hamera, 347–50. Thousand Oaks, CA: Sage Publications.

– 2013. *Cultural Struggles: Performance, Ethnography, Praxis*. Edited by E. Patrick Johnson. Ann Arbor: University of Michigan Press.

Conrad, Diane H. 2008. *The Sage Encyclopedia of Qualitative Research Methods*. Edited by Lisa Given. Thousand Oaks, CA: Sage Publications.

Couser, G. Thomas. 2005. "Disability and (Auto)Ethnography." *Journal of Contemporary Ethnography* 34 (2): 121–42. https://doi.org/10.1177/0891241604272089.

– 2011. "Introduction: Disability and Life Writing." *Journal of Literary & Cultural Disability Studies* 5 (3): 229–41. https://doi.org/10.3828/jlcds.2011.20.

Cowan, T.L., and Jasmine Rault. 2014. "The Labour of Being Studied in a Free Love Economy." *Ephemera: Theory & Politics in Organization* 14 (3): 471–88.

Cox, Aimee Meredith. 2015. *Shapeshifters: Black Girls and the Choreography of Citizenship*. Durham, NC: Duke University Press.

Craft, Renée Alexander, Meida Mcneal, Mshaï S. Mwangola, and Queen Meccasia E. Zabriskie. 2007. "The Quilt: Towards a Twenty-First-Century Black Feminist Ethnography." *Performance Research* 12 (3): 55–73. https://doi.org/10.1080/13528160701771311.

"Cripping the Arts Conference Access Guide." 2019. Toronto: Tangled Art+Disability. https://tangledarts.org/events/cripping-the-arts-2019/.

Davidson, Michael. 2016. "Cleavings: Critical Losses in the Politics of Gain." *Disability Studies Quarterly* 36 (2). https://doi.org/10.18061/dsq.v36i2.4287.

Denzin, Norman K. 2003. *Performance Ethnography: Critical Pedagogy and the Politics of Culture*. Thousand Oaks, CA: Sage Publications.

Dokumaçi, Arseli. 2016. "Affordance Creations of Disability Performance: Limits of a Disabled Theater." *Theatre Research in Canada* 37 (2). https://journals.lib.unb.ca/index.php/TRIC/article/view/25321.

– 2017. "Vital Affordances, Occupying Niches: An Ecological Approach to Disability and Performance." *Research in Drama Education: The Journal of Applied Theatre and Performance* 22 (3): 393–412. https://doi.org/10.1080/13569783.2017.1326808.

Dorwart, Jason. 2016. "I Was Never Alone: Translating Ethnography into Accessibility." *TheatreForum* 50: 4–5.

– 2017. "The Incorporeal Corpse: Disability, Liminality, Performance." PhD diss., University of California, San Diego. https://search.proquest.com/docview/1910117286/abstract/39D8F239EC5A47A8PQ/1.

Dugdale, Sasha. 2009. "Preface." In *Performing Violence: Literary and Theatrical Experiments of New Russian Drama*, edited by Birgit Beumers and M.N. Lipovetsky, 13–26. Bristol, UK: Intellect.

Elliott, Denielle, and Dara Culhane. 2017. *A Different Kind of Ethnography: Imaginative Practices and Creative Methodologies*. Toronto: University of Toronto Press.

Erevelles, Nirmala. 2011. *Disability and Difference in Global Contexts: Enabling a Transformative Body Politic*. New York: Palgrave Macmillan.

Escobar, Arturo. 2018. *Designs for the Pluriverse: Radical Interdependence, Autonomy, and the Making of Worlds*. Durham, NC: Duke University Press.

Fabian, Johannes. 1990. *Power and Performance: Ethnographic Explorations through Proverbial Wisdom and Theater in Shaba, Zaire*. New Directions in Anthropological Writing. Madison: University of Wisconsin Press.

– 2000. *Out of Our Minds: Reason and Madness in the Exploration of Central Africa: The Ad. E. Jensen Lectures at the Frobenius Institut, University of Frankfurt*. Berkeley: University of California Press.

– (1983) 2014. *Time and the Other: How Anthropology Makes Its Object*. New York: Columbia University Press.

Fehérváry, Krisztina. 2013. *Politics in Color and Concrete: Socialist Materialities and the Middle Class in Hungary*. New Anthropologies of Europe. Bloomington: Indiana University Press.

Field, Deborah A. 2007. *Private Life and Communist Morality in Khrushchev's Russia*. New York: Peter Lang.

Fischer-Lichte, Erika, Ramona Mosse, and Minou Arjomand. 2014. *The Routledge Introduction to Theatre and Performance Studies*. English Language edition. London: Routledge.

Fox, Ann M., and Joan Lipkin. 2011. "Res(Crip)ting Feminist Theater through Disability Theater: Selections from the DisAbility Project." In *Feminist Disability Studies*, edited by Kim Q. Hall, 287–310. Bloomington: Indiana University Press .

Frank, Gelya. 2000. *Venus on Wheels: Two Decades of Dialogue on Disability, Biography, and Being Female in America*. Berkeley: University of California Press.

Fraser, Nancy, and Linda Gordon. 1994. "A Genealogy of Dependency: Tracing a Keyword of the U.S. Welfare State." *Signs* 19 (2): 309–36. https://doi.org/10.1086/494886.

Freedman, John, ed. 2014. *Real and Phantom Pains: An Anthology of New Russian Drama*. Washington, DC: New Academia Publishing.

– 2017. "The Show Trial of a Russian Theater Director (Op-Ed)." *Moscow Times,* 25 August. http://themoscowtimes.com/articles/show-trial-kirill-serebrennikov-58759.

– 2018a. "A Revolutionary Road: Remembering Mikhail Ugarov, the Father of Russia's Radical New Drama Movement." *The Calvert Journal*, 7 April. https://www.calvertjournal.com/articles/show/9852/mikhail-ugarov-remembering-the-father-of-russias-new-drama-movement.

– 2018b. "With Yelena Gremina's Death, Teatr.Doc Enters a New Era." *Moscow Times*, 17 May. http://themoscowtimes.com/articles/with-yelena-greminas-death-teatrdoc-enters-a-new-era-61476.

Freeman, Barry. 2017. *Staging Strangers: Theatre and Global Ethics*. Montreal and Kingston: McGill-Queen's University Press.

Friedner, Michele Ilana. 2015. *Valuing Deaf Worlds in Urban India*. New Brunswick, NJ: Rutgers University Press.

Friedner, Michele, and Tyler Zoanni. 2018. "Disability from the South: Toward a Lexicon." Somatosphere. http://somatosphere.net/2018/12/disability-from-the-south-toward-a-lexicon.html.

Fukuyama, Francis. 1989. "The End of History?" *The National Interest* 16: 3–18.

– 2012. "The Future of History: Can Liberal Democracy Survive the Decline of the Middle Class?" *Foreign Affairs*, 53–61.

Galloway, Terry, Donna Marie Nudd, and Carrie Sandahl. 2007. "'Actual Lives' and the Ethic of Accommodation." In *The Community Performance*

Reader, edited by Petra Kuppers and Gwen Robertson, 227–34. New York: Routledge.

Galmarini-Kabala, Maria Cristina. 2016. *The Right to Be Helped: Deviance, Entitlement, and the Soviet Moral Order*. DeKalb, IL: NIU Press.

Garland-Thomson, Rosemarie. 1997. *Extraordinary Bodies: Figuring Physical Disability in American Culture and Literature*. New York: Columbia University Press.

– 2002. "Politics of Staring: Visual Rhetorics of Disability in Popular Photography." In *Disability Studies: Enabling the Humanities*, edited by Sharon L. Snyder, Brenda Jo Brueggemann, and Rosemarie Garland-Thomson, 56–75. New York: Modern Language Association of America.

– 2005. "Dares to Stares: Disabled Women Performance Artists & the Dynamics of Staring." In *Bodies in Commotion: Disability & Performance*, edited by Carrie Sandahl and Philip Auslander, 30–41. Ann Arbor: University of Michigan Press.

– 2017. *Extraordinary Bodies: Figuring Physical Disability in American Culture and Literature*. 20th anniversary ed. New York: Columbia University Press.

Geertz, Clifford. 1973. *The Interpretation of Cultures*. New York: Basic Books.

Gennep, Arnold van. 1960. *The Rites of Passage*. London: Routledge and Paul.

Gill, Carol J. 1995. "A Psychological View of Disability Culture." *Disability Studies Quarterly* 15 (4): 16–19.

Gille, Zsuzsa. 2010. "Is There a Global Postsocialist Condition?" *Global Society* 24 (1): 9–30. https://doi.org/10.1080/13600820903431953.

Ginsburg, Faye, and Rayna Rapp. 2013. "Disability Worlds." *Annual Review of Anthropology* 42 (1): 53–68. https://doi.org/10.1146/annurev-anthro-092412-155502.

Giordano, Cristiana, and Greg Pierotti. 2018. "Dramaturgy." Edited by Cassandra Hartblay, Joseph D. Hankins, and Melissa L. Caldwell. Keywords for Ethnography & Design, *Cultural Anthropology*. https://culanth.org/fieldsights/dramaturgy.

Grech, Shaun. 2015. "Decolonising Eurocentric Disability Studies: Why Colonialism Matters in the Disability and Global South Debate." *Social Identities* 21 (1): 6–21. https://doi.org/10.1080/13504630.2014.995347.

– 2016. "Disability and Development: Critical Connections, Gaps and Contradictions." In *Disability in the Global South: The Critical Handbook*, edited by Shaun Grech and Karen Soldatic, 3–19. Cham, Switzerland: Springer International Publishing.

Hartblay, Cassandra. 2014. "Welcome to Sergeichburg: Disability, Crip Performance, and the Comedy of Recognition in Russia." *The Journal of Social Policy Studies* 12 (1): 111–25.

– 2015. "'Body Leads': Medicalizing Cultural Difference, or, What Are We Doing When We Say Putin Has Asperger's Syndrome?" *Somatosphere*, 17 February. http://somatosphere.net/2015/02/putin-aspergers.html.

– 2017. "Good Ramps, Bad Ramps: Centralized Design Standards and Disability Access in Urban Russian Infrastructure." *American Ethnologist* 44 (1): 9–22. https://doi.org/10.1111/amet.12422.

– 2019. "After Marginalization: Pixelization, Disability, and Social Difference in Digital Russia." *South Atlantic Quarterly* 118 (3): 543–72. https://doi.org/10.1215/00382876-7616151.

– 2020. "Disability Expertise: Claiming Disability Anthropology." *Current Anthropology*, Wenner-Gren Symposium Series, no. S21 (February).

Hartblay, Cassandra, Joseph D. Hankins, and Melissa L. Caldwell, eds. 2018. "Keywords for Ethnography and Design." *Society for Cultural Anthropology*, 29 March. https://culanth.org/fieldsights/introduction-keywords-for-ethnography-and-design.

Helderman, Rosalind S., Moriah Balingit, Shane Harris, and Tom Hamburger. 2018. "Before Her Arrest as an Alleged Russian Agent, Maria Butina's Proud Defense of Her Homeland Drew Notice at American University." *Washington Post*, 25 July. https://www.washingtonpost.com/politics/before-her-arrest-as-an-alleged-russian-agent-maria-butinas-proud-defense-of-her-homeland-drew-notice-at-american-university/2018/07/25/957c1812-8c2a-11e8-a345-a1bf7847b375_story.html.

Henderson, Bruce, and Noam Ostrander, eds. 2010. *Understanding Disability Studies and Performance Studies*. 1st ed. London: Routledge.

Iarskaia-Smirnova, Elena. 2001. "Social Change and Self Empowerment: Stories of Disabled People in Russia." In *Disability and the Life Course: Global Perspectives*, edited by Mark Priestley, 101–12. New York: Cambridge University Press.

Ingstad, Benedicte, and Susan Whyte. 1995. *Disability and Culture*. Berkeley: University of California Press.

Ingstad, Benedicte, and Susan Reynolds Whyte. 2007. *Disability in Local and Global Worlds*. Berkeley: University of California Press.

Janney, Matt. 2017. "Gogol Centre Theatre Director Kirill Serebrennikov Arrested in Fraud Investigation." *The Calvert Journal*. 22 August. https://www.calvertjournal.com/news/show/8822/kirill-serebrennikov-detained-ongoing-fraud-investigation.

Johnson, E. Patrick. 2008. *Sweet Tea: Black Gay Men of the South*. Chapel Hill: University of North Carolina Press.

– 2020. *Sweet Tea: A Play*. Chicago: Northwestern University Press.

Johnson, E. Patrick, ed. 2013. *Cultural Struggles: Performance, Ethnography, Praxis*. Ann Arbor: University of Michigan Press.

Johnston, Kirsty. 2012. *Stage Turns: Canadian Disability Theatre*. Montreal: McGill-Queen's University Press.

– 2016. *Disability Theatre and Modern Drama: Recasting Modernism*. London: Bloomsbury Publishing.

Kafer, Alison. 2003. "Compulsory Bodies: Reflections on Heterosexuality and Able-Bodiedness." *Journal of Women's History* 15 (3): 77–89. https://doi .org/10.1353/jowh.2003.0071.

– 2013. *Feminist, Queer, Crip*. Bloomington: Indiana University Press.

Kayiatos, Anastasia. 2010. "Sooner Speaking Than Silent, Sooner Silent Than Mute: Soviet Deaf Theatre and Pantomime after Stalin." *Theatre Survey* 51 (1): 5–31. https://doi.org/10.1017/S0040557410000207.

– 2013. "Global Gays/Local Crips: Or, Why Neoliberalism Needs Russia's Orphans 'Retarded.'" Paper presented at Troubling Discourses of Development I: Cripping Development Conference, Charles University, Prague, Czech Republic, 20 September.

Kazubowski-Houston, Magdalena. 2015. *Staging Strife: Lessons from Performing Ethnography with Polish Roma Women*. First paperback edition. Montreal and Kingston: McGill-Queen's University Press.

Kikkas, Kaido. 2001. "Lifting the Iron Curtain." In *Disability and the Life Course: Global Perspectives*, edited by Mark Priestley, 113–22. New York: Cambridge University Press.

Kim, Eunjung. 2014. "The Specter of Vulnerability and Disabled Bodies in Protest." In *Disability, Human Rights and the Limits of Humanitarianism*, edited by Michael Carl Gill and Cathy J. Schlund-Vials, 137–54. Farnham, UK: Ashgate.

– 2017. *Curative Violence: Rehabilitating Disability, Gender, and Sexuality in Modern Korea*. Durham, NC: Duke University Press.

Kohrman, Matthew. 2005. *Bodies of Difference: Experiences of Disability and Institutional Advocacy in the Making of Modern China*. Berkeley: University of California Press.

Kolářová, Kateřina. 2015. "'Grandpa Lives in Paradise Now': Biological Precarity and the Global Economy of Debility." *Feminist Review* 111 (1): 75–87. https://doi.org/10.1057/fr.2015.45.

Kolářová, Kateřina, and M. Katharina Wiedlack. 2016. "Crip Notes on the Idea of Development." *Somatechnics* 6 (2): 125–41. https://doi.org /10.3366/soma.2016.0187.

Kulick, Don. 1998. *Travesti: Sex, Gender, and Culture among Brazilian Transgendered Prostitutes*. Chicago: University of Chicago Press.

Kulick, Don, and Jens Rydström. 2015. *Loneliness and Its Opposite: Sex, Disability, and the Ethics of Engagement*. Durham, NC: Duke University Press.

Kuppers, Petra. 2014a. "Crip Time." *Tikkun* 29 (4): 29–30. https://doi .org/10.1215/08879982-2810062.

– 2014b. *Studying Disability Arts and Culture: An Introduction*. New York: Palgrave Macmillan.

– 2017. *Theatre & Disability*. New York: Red Globe Press.

Landsman, Gail. 2009. *Reconstructing Motherhood and Disability in the Age of "Perfect" Babies*. New York: Routledge.

Lemon, Alaina. 2008. "Hermeneutic Algebra: Solving for Love, Time/Space, and Value in Putin-Era Personal Ads." *Journal of Linguistic Anthropology* 18 (2): 236–67. https://doi.org/10.1111/j.1548-1395.2008.00021.x.

Lewis, Victoria Ann. 2004. "The Theatrical Landscape of Disability." *Disability Studies Quarterly* 24 (3). https://doi.org/10.18061/dsq.v24i3.511.

Linton, Simi. 1998. *Claiming Disability: Knowledge and Identity*. New York: New York University Press.

– 2005. "What Is Disability Studies?" *PMLA* 120 (2): 518–22. https://www.jstor.org/stable/25486177.

Lipovetsky, Mark, and Birgit Beumers. 2008. "Reality Performance: Documentary Trends in Post-Soviet Russian Theatre." *Contemporary Theatre Review* 18 (3): 293–306. https://doi.org/10.1080/10486800802123583.

Madison, D. Soyini. 2006. "Dwight Conquergood's 'Rethinking Ethnography.'" In *The Sage Handbook of Performance Studies*, edited by D. Soyini Madison and Judith Hamera, 347–50. Thousand Oaks, CA: Sage Publications.

– 2012. *Critical Ethnography: Method, Ethics, and Performance*. 2nd ed. Thousand Oaks, CA: Sage Publications.

Malinowski, Bronislaw. 1984. *Argonauts of the Western Pacific: An Account of Native Enterprise and Adventure in the Archipelagoes of Melanesian New Guinea*. Prospect Heights, IL: Waveland Press.

Matza, Tomas. 2009. "MOSCOW'S ECHO: Technologies of the Self, Publics, and Politics on the Russian Talk Show." *Cultural Anthropology* 24 (3): 489–522. https://doi.org/10.1111/j.1548-1360.2009.01038.x.

– 2018. *Shock Therapy: Psychology, Precarity, and Well-Being in Postsocialist Russia*. Durham, NC: Duke University Press.

McRuer, Robert. 2002. "Compulsory Able-Bodiedness and Queer/Disabled Existence." *Disability Studies: Enabling the Humanities*, edited by Rosemarie Garland-Thomson, Brenda Jo Brueggemann, and Sharon L. Snyder, 88–99. New York: MLA Publications.

Meekosha, Helen, and Karen Soldatic. 2011. "Human Rights and the Global South: The Case of Disability." *Third World Quarterly* 32 (8): 1383–97. https://doi.org/10.1080/01436597.2011.614800.

Megel, Joseph. 2014. *Sweet Tea: Black Gay Men of the South: A New Play*. Play Performance. Durham Arts Council, Durham, NC. https://vimeo.com/89185412.

Merry, Sally Engle. 2006. "Anthropology and International Law." *Annual Review of Anthropology* 35 (1): 99–116. https://doi.org/10.1146/annurev.anthro.35.081705.123245.

Miroshnik, Meg. 2014. *The Fairytale Lives of Russian Girls (or, Devushka)*. Samuel French Acting Edition. New York: Concord Theatricals.

Mitchell, David, and Sharon L. Snyder. 2001. *Narrative Prosthesis: Disability and the Dependencies of Discourse*. Ann Arbor: University of Michigan Press.

Moser, Ingunn, and John Law. 1999. "Good Passages, Bad Passages." *The Sociological Review* 46 (2): 196–219. https://doi.org/10.1111/1467-954X.46.s.11.

Murphy, Keith M. 2016. "Design and Anthropology." *Annual Review of Anthropology*, 45: 433–49.

Nakamura, Karen. 2006. *Deaf in Japan: Signing and the Politics of Identity.* Ithaca, NY: Cornell University Press.

Narayan, Kirin. 2012. *Alive in the Writing: Crafting Ethnography in the Company of Chekhov.* Chicago: University of Chicago Press.

OED Online. n.d. "Vulnerable, Adj." Accessed 2 October 2019. http://www.oed.com/view/Entry/224872#eid15169124.

Pandian, Anand. 2012. "The Time of Anthropology: Notes from a Field of Contemporary Experience." *Cultural Anthropology* 27 (4): 547–71. https://doi.org/10.1111/j.1548-1360.2012.01161.x.

Parker, Patricia, Dorothy Holland, Jean Dennison, Sara H. Smith, and Melvin Jackson. 2018. "Decolonizing the Academy: Lessons from the Graduate Certificate in Participatory Research at the University of North Carolina at Chapel Hill." *Qualitative Inquiry* 24 (7): 464–77. https://doi.org/10.1177/1077800417729846.

Peters, Susan. 2000. "Is There a Disability Culture? A Syncretisation of Three Possible World Views." *Disability & Society* 15 (4): 583–601. https://doi.org/10.1080/09687590050058198.

Petryna, Adriana. 2002. *Life Exposed: Biological Citizens after Chernobyl.* Princeton: Princeton University Press.

Phillips, Sarah. 2011. *Disability and Mobile Citizenship in Postsocialist Ukraine.* Bloomington: Indiana University Press.

Piepzna-Samarasinha, Leah Lakshmi. 2018. *Care Work: Dreaming Disability Justice.* Vancouver: Arsenal Pulp Press.

Pink, Sarah. 2015. *Doing Sensory Ethnography.* 2nd ed. Thousand Oaks, CA: Sage Publications.

Pollock, Della. 1998. "Performing Writing." In *The Ends of Performance*, edited by Ann O'Day Maples, Peggy Phelan, and Jill Lane, 73–103. New York: New York University Press.

– 2006. "Marking New Directions in Performance Ethnography." *Text and Performance Quarterly* 26 (4): 325–9. https://doi.org/10.1080/10462930600828733.

Price, Margaret. 2011. *Mad at School: Rhetorics of Mental Disability and Academic Life.* Ann Arbor: University of Michigan Press.

Priestley, Mark, ed. 2001. *Disability and the Life Course: Global Perspectives.* New York: Cambridge University Press.

Puar, Jasbir K. 2017. *The Right to Maim: Debility, Capacity, Disability.* Durham, NC: Duke University Press.

Ralph, Laurence. 2020. "Torture without Torturers." *Current Anthropology*, Wenner-Gren Symposium Series 61 (S21): S87–S96. https://doi.org/10.1086/705574

Rapp, Rayna, and Faye Ginsburg. 2001. "Enabling Disability: Rewriting Kinship, Reimagining Citizenship." *Public Culture* 13 (3): 533–56. https:// doi.org/10.1215/08992363-13-3-533.
– 2011. "Reverberations: Disability and the New Kinship Imaginary." *Anthropological Quarterly* 84 (2): 379–410. https://doi.org/10.1353 /anq.2011.0030.
Rasell, Michael, and Elena Iarskaia-Smirnova, eds. 2013. *Disability in Eastern Europe and the Former Soviet Union: History, Policy and Everyday Life*. New York: Routledge.
Rayfield, Donald. 2000. *Anton Chekhov: A Life*. Evanston, IL: Northwestern University Press.
Rich, Adrienne. 1980. "Compulsory Heterosexuality and Lesbian Existence." *Signs: Journal of Women in Culture and Society* 5 (4): 631–60. https://doi .org/10.1086/493756.
Ries, Nancy. 1997. *Russian Talk: Culture and Conversation during Perestroika*. Ithaca, NY: Cornell University Press.
Robbins, Joel. 2013. "Beyond the Suffering Subject: Toward an Anthropology of the Good." *Journal of the Royal Anthropological Institute* 19 (3): 447–62. https://doi.org/10.1111/1467-9655.12044.
Roudakova, Natalia. 2017. *Losing Pravda: Ethics and the Press in Post-Truth Russia*. Cambridge: Cambridge University Press.
Ryazanov, Eldar, director, and Emil Braginsky. 2001. *Ironia sudby, ili, S lekhim parom (The Irony of Fate, or Enjoy Your Bath!)*. DVD. Moscow: Mosfilm.
Samuels, Ellen. 2017. "Six Ways of Looking at Crip Time." *Disability Studies Quarterly* 37 (3). https://doi.org/10.18061/dsq.v37i3.5824.
Sandahl, Carrie. 1999. "Ahhhh Freak out! Metaphors of Disability and Femaleness in Performance." *Theatre Topics* 9 (1): 11–30. https://doi .org/10.1353/tt.1999.0006.
– 2000. "Bob Flanagan: Taking It like a Man." *Journal of Dramatic Theory and Criticism* 15 (1): 97–106. https://journals.ku.edu/jdtc/article /view/3354.
– 2005. "The Tyranny of Neutral: Disability and Actor Training." *Bodies in Commotion: Disability and Performance*, edited by Carrie Sandahl and Philip Auslander, 255–67. Ann Arbor: University of Michigan Press.
Satz, Ani B. 2015. "Vulnerability." In *Keywords for Disability Studies*, edited by Rachel Adams, Benjamin Reiss, and David Serlin, 185–6. New York: New York University Press.
Schechner, Richard. 2004. "Performance Studies: A Broad Spectrum Approach." In *The Performance Studies Reader*, edited by Henry Bial, 7–9. London: Routledge.
Scheer, Jessica. 1994. "Culture and Disability: An Anthropological Point of View." In *Human Diversity: Perspectives on People in Context*, edited by Edison J. Trickett, Roderick J. Watts, and Dina Birman, 244–60. San Francisco: Jossey-Bass.

Serebrennikov, Kirill. 2009. "Foreword." In *Performing Violence: Literary and Theatrical Experiments of New Russian Drama*, edited by Birgit Beumers and M.N. Lipovetsky, 9–12. Chicago: Intellect.

Siegelbaum, Lewis H., ed. 2006. *Borders of Socialism: Private Spheres of Soviet Russia*. New York: Palgrave Macmillan.

Sins Invalid. 2015. "Disability Justice: A Working Draft by Patty Berne." 9 June. Accessed 28 April 2020. https://www.sinsinvalid.org/blog/disability-justice-a-working-draft-by-patty-berne.

Spiegel, Alix. n.d. "The New Norm." Invisibilia from NPR. Accessed 5 September 2018. https://www.npr.org/programs/invisibilia/481887848/the-new-norm?showDate=2016-06-17.

Suchland, Jennifer. 2011. "Is Postsocialism Transnational?" *Signs: Journal of Women in Culture and Society* 36 (4): 837–62. https://doi.org/10.1086/658899.

Temple, Emily. 2018. "'Write a Sentence as Clean as a Bone' and Other Advice from James Baldwin." *Literary Hub* (blog). 2 August. https://lithub.com/write-a-sentence-as-clean-as-a-bone-and-other-advice-from-james-baldwin/.

Titchkosky, Tanya. 2011. *The Question of Access: Disability, Space, Meaning*. Toronto: University of Toronto Press.

Trouillot, Michel-Rolph. 2003. "Anthropology and the Savage Slot: The Poetics and Politics of Otherness." In *Global Transformations*, 7–28. New York: Palgrave Macmillan.

Turner, Edith, ed. 2012. *Communitas: The Anthropology of Collective Joy*. New York: Palgrave Macmillan.

Turner, Victor. 1967. *The Forest of Symbols: Aspects of Ndembu Ritual*. Ithaca, NY: Cornell University Press.

– 1982. *From Ritual to Theatre: The Human Seriousness of Play*. New York: PAJ Publicaitons.

– 1988. *The Anthropology of Performance*. Performance Studies Series 4. New York: PAJ Publications.

– 1995. *The Ritual Process: Structure and Anti-Structure*. New York: Aldine de Gruyter.

Turner, Victor, and Edith Turner. 1982. "Performing Ethnography." *TDR: The Drama Review* 26 (2): 33–50. https://doi.org/10.2307/1145429.

Von Geldern, James. 1995. *Mass Culture in Soviet Russia: Tales, Poems, Songs, Movies, Plays, and Folklore, 1917–1953*. Bloomington: Indiana University Press.

Weygandt, Susanna. 2016. "The Structure of Plasticity: Resistance and Accommodation in Russian New Drama." *TDR: The Drama Review* 60 (1): 116–31. https://doi.org/10.1162/DRAM_a_00527.

– 2018. "Revisiting Skaz in Ivan Vyrypaev's Cinema and Theatre: Rhythms and Sounds of Postdramatic Rap." *Studies in Russian and Soviet Cinema* 12 (3): 195–214. https://doi.org/10.1080/17503132.2018.1511260.

Wiedlack, M. Katharina, and Masha Neufeld. 2016. "Dangerous and Moving? Disability, Russian Popular Culture and North/Western Hegemony." *Somatechnics* 6 (2): 216–34.

Wool, Zoë Hamilton. 2015. *After War: The Weight of Life at Walter Reed.* Durham, NC: Duke University Press. https://doi.org/10.3366/soma.2016.0192.

Young, Allan. 1995. *The Harmony of Illusions: Inventing Post-Traumatic Stress Disorder.* Princeton: Princeton University Press.

Yurchak, Alexei. 2006. *Everything Was Forever, until It Was No More: The Last Soviet Generation.* Princeton: Princeton University Press.

Zvyagintsev, Andrey, director. 2015. *Leviathan.* Russian with English subtitles. Produced by Aleksandr Rodnyansky. DVD. Sony Pictures Home Entertainment.

Appendixes

Appendix 1: Performance Ethnography Exercises

These exercises are intended as prompts for those interested in the process of developing a play script in the model of *I Was Never Alone*, or who would like to experiment with different modes of developing ethnographic data. The exercises may be assigned or facilitated in a classroom or workshop setting as a learning exercise about documentary or accessible theater, or, may be read as an invitation to experiment with ethnographic practice. Some exercises will be more interesting for a given reader than others. Some may be obvious to one reader, but new to someone else approaching this text from a different disciplinary perspective. Take what works for you.

These exercises are not meant to deliver a reliable result. This is an interpretive, expressive, improvisational, experimental process, not a positivist statement about a "right" way to do things. Humans learn through performative play. In embodied action, we come to know differently. Playful experimentation allows us to improvise (Dumit et al. 2018), and find new configurations of the social (words, social roles, identities, interactions, etc.). Some of these are exercises that I use in my own Ethnographic Methods courses, while others I have tried with graduate and faculty working groups. In general, they are my own interpretations that build on the working methods of other performance ethnographers, especially informed by my training in performance ethnography at the University of North Carolina Chapel Hill. I encourage all readers to explore those texts and theorize the ways in which different methodological choices produce different processes and performative experiences.

EXERCISE ONE: OBSERVATIONAL WRITING

Prompt:

As a group, from a home base, take a ten-to-fifteen minute walk around the surrounding proximity. Do not talk. Proceed together as a group. Whether it is a familiar or new place, use all of your senses to take in the world around you. Absorb details that you will write down once you return to your home base. Pay attention to sounds, smells, conversations, colors, the ordinary and the unusual. Use your own body as your interpretive instrument, a sensory organ that observes, remembers, records, and interprets – reliably and unreliably.

When you return to home base, without talking, go directly to a place to sit and write. Write down what you have observed during the walk. Spend ten to fifteen minutes writing without stopping. Be as descriptive as possible.

When the time is up, share what you've come up with. Some participants might wish to read their writing or sections of their writing out loud. Others might only be willing to answer a few questions.

Consider the following:
- What did you write about?
- Are any things that everyone wrote about?
- That only one person wrote about?
- How did you decide what to write about?
- What formats did you use to record your ideas quickly – full sentences, jotted disjointed phrases, bullet points, quotations from overheard conversations?
- Was there anything you forgot? What was the experience of memory like?
- How did you decide what order to record things in first?
- How did your understanding of what you observed change in the writing?
- Did you tend to focus on things seen, heard, or otherwise felt?
- Did your own writerly voice emerge in your written text? Why or why not?

EXERCISE TWO: PLAYING WITH INTERVIEW TRANSCRIPTION

Prompt:

Interview a family member, friend, colleague, or classmate. You might work in a small group.

A question that I've used in the past to prompt a dramatic narrative to record is this:

Close your eyes. Imagine your fourteen year old self. [pause]

In your mind's eye, look around. Where is your fourteen year old self? What is your fourteen year old self wearing? Describe what your fourteen year old self looks like, what your fourteen year old self is doing. If you, today, could give a message to your fourteen year old self, what would it be?

Transcribe the interview. Then, in a group, consider the transcription. How might you stage this scene? What props, costumes, sound effects, pacing, tone might you use, and how would changing these elements shift the meaning of the monologue?

Perform the scene for an audience of peers.

Consider the following:
• How did the story transform from voice to audio recording?
  ... from audio recording to written text?
  ... from written text to performance?
• During the interview, the transcription, or the performance, what was too personal to share?
• Where did representation fail, and where did it succeed?

EXERCISE THREE: CAST OF CHARACTERS

Prompt:

Review the Cast of Characters in *I Was Never Alone*.

Thinking of your own field site, make a list of characters who would appear in a rendition of your research staged as a play. Write a brief, one-paragraph description of each character.

Consider the following:
• Who are the main characters?

- Which characters are named, and which are known only by their relational or occupational designations?
- What clothes might they wear?
- How might a stranger be made familiar through a description of their mannerisms?
- What kinds of descriptors would you prefer to avoid? How do your characters align with or depart from popular stereotypes associated with their identities?

EXERCISE FOUR: PRELIMINARY SCENIC COMPONENTS LIST

Prompt:

Review the prop list (Appendix 5) and scene descriptions at the start of each portrait in *I Was Never Alone*.

Thinking of your own field site (or cast of characters, above) consider each scene or character in turn. Do a quick brainstorm to create a list of objects that might appear in each character portrait. **Complete a written list of possible props and set items for one or more scenes.**

Consider the following:
- What objects, furniture, and decor remind you of a particular person? Of a particular place where you conducted an interview with that person?
- How do the objects in a scene description root a scene in time and place?
- Are there several locations that might be collapsed into a composite location?
- Or, would an interview that actually took place in one place or multiple locales be more effectively dramatized if set elsewhere?

EXERCISE FIVE: MEDIA FOR THEATER

Prompt:

Make a list of sounds and media that might come up in the course of each scene, or as transitions between scenes. **Complete a written list of possible audio-visual items for one or more scenes.**

Consider the following:

- Are there songs, videos, pieces of writing, or other cultural texts that your interlocutors talked about, showed to you, or kept close at hand? Which media "go with" each character?
- Are there songs, videos, pieces of writing, or other cultural texts that your interlocutor authored?
- How does including a variety of sensory formats enrich a theatrical experience?
- Which elements may be accessible or inaccessible to audience members with different sensory experiences?

EXERCISE SIX: AN ETHNOGRAPHIC SCENE

Prompt:

Review the scene descriptions at the start of each portrait in *I Was Never Alone*. You may also wish to consider scene descriptions in other contemporary play scripts. Drawing on your own research material and these genre examples, **craft the introductory text for one or more ethnographic scenes.**

Consider the following:

- What is specific about the writerly style of scene descriptions?
- How do scene descriptions differ from descriptions in ethnographic prose?
- What tools will the imagined reader of a play script/ethnographic text have to interpret scenic details?
- How might directors, dramaturgs, actors, lighting designers, set designers, students, ethnographers, and general readers interpret the same scene description differently?

EXERCISE SEVEN: WRITING A MONOLOGUE-PORTRAIT FOR PERFORMANCE

Step One: Select a transcribed interview from your own ethnographic archive.

Step Two: Identify dramatic potential.

Read through the transcript. Are there dramatic moments already there? For instance, moments when an emotive constellation is revealed, or a particular narrative idea gets developed? Or, are there particularly funny moments, or places where the narrator is intentionally making you (the interviewer) laugh? Start from these paragraphs.

Step Three: Translation.

If your interviews are in a language other than the language of performance/scholarship, now your work of translation begins.

As you translate, beginning from the moments of emotional or humorous energy, try to capture the particular idiosyncrasies of voice and tone that your narrator brings to the scene. Are they sarcastic? Eager to please? Witty? Wry? Withholding? Imagine that you are going to cast a famous actor to play them? Who would you cast to capture their voice? To what extent will you retain the tics of real time human speech – likes, um, etc.?

Step Four: Select the main narrative arc of the portrait.

Center the portrait around revealing some fundamental truth about the narrator – their feelings about a social or familial relationship, their sense of their own identity in society, etc. The narrator's own intention and the ultimate meaning of the narrative may not match – for instance, in IWNA, Anya sets out to talk about her new apartment, and over the course of the narrative, it turns out that her apartment acts as a proxy for her relationship with her father and her fears about what will happen to her as a disabled person when her parents die. Craft the narrative around this type of dramatic contradiction. Inevitably, you will have to select some aspect of a person's life story to draw out and highlight, while leaving other aspects undeveloped.

Step Five: Try reading the portrait aloud.

Check for pacing, translation, consistency, and clarity. Verbatim speech may be long, round about, or repetitive. There may be references to previous interviews, other people, or ideas that need clarification for a reader/audience unfamiliar with the narrator. Or, there might be long segments of text that seem to get boring: can you add an interjection of some kind (a phone ringing, a side conversation, a motion or action)? Cut out extraneous asides, or add in clarifying phrases. Look for places where you must add stage directions to make meaning and pacing clear. But, resist the anthropological temptation to direct every movement and facial expression from within the text of the script. What interesting performative moments and interpretive insights might come from trusting the director and actors?

Step Six: Experiment with how you represent the word on the page.

There are a great many styles of transcription, each with different affordances. Formal transcription conventions for linguistic analysis, for instance, are not particularly useful for theater scripts. But, you might play with line breaks, italics, and stage directions as different ways to indicate how a reader of the script might imagine the storytelling as live performance. Consider the various genre conventions and idiosyncrasies of theater scripts. As you develop the work, you might research and think with performance traditions popular in the region where your research was conducted. Is there a performance style that is particularly culturally meaningful that might enter in to your representation?

Step Seven: Place and relationships.

Review where you have set the portrait in space, and how you have brought the character to life through relationships with other people and objects around them. Who is the main character of the portrait in relation to others? Experiment with dialogue, relationships, setting, and possibilities therein.

Step Eight: Locating the ethnographer in the scene.

Where is the ethnographer in the portrait? One of the challenges of ethnographic theater is deciding how you will treat the ethnographer in the play. Will the ethnographer be implied only? Appear as a background character that reads the scene descriptions? Appear as a central character whose narrative journey anchors the script in some way?

EXERCISE EIGHT: FROM TEXT TO VOICE – THE TABLE READING

Organize a table reading, an event in which others read your script aloud, while you listen and take notes.

A table reading is part of a script development process, not a performance. There is no stage, no blocking, or movement. Often the actors are reading the script sight unseen. Sometimes actors will have a week or two with the script to read through it in advance. It is a way for you as a playwright to work out a draft of a script. For ethnographers, this is a useful stage at which to collaborate with a theater director or other playwrights developing new work.

Hearing a work read out loud by another person is essential to understand how a script works or does not work as a performed piece of theater. Listening to another person read a script draft out loud brings up numerous questions. Take notes on your copy of the draft script.

What sounds right for a given character and what sounds "wrong"? Are there moments when a scene feels flat or boring or a character goes on too long about one topic? Moments when a character comes alive? Does each character have a unique voice? What is a particular actor or reader getting "right" or "wrong" about the voice of the character as you have adapted and envisioned it? Where can you add or subtract stage directions, extra words, etc.?

Pause after reading each section and ask for feedback from the group. What is clear about the narrative? What is murky? Where is it dragging? Where does it move too quickly? Attending to this kind of pacing will make the script appealing to actors and directors who might perform it.

Following the table reading, review your mark ups and notes. Catalog the changes that you need to make, and revise your draft script accordingly.

Appendix 2: Disability Terminology

As with many politically disenfranchised groups, people with disabilities involved in self-advocacy have devoted a great deal of time and attention to observing the ways that dominant ideas about disability as an undesirable weakness are frequently reproduced through taken for granted turns of phrase. Taking the time to think about how and where ableism lurks in daily language is an important step for allies and those learning about disability politics. In general, preferred language is not always agreed upon within activist and scholarly circles, and also tends to change very quickly. This partial list of terms reflects the moment of publication, and should be taken as a description or snapshot of a cultural moment, rather than as a prescriptive statement for the future.

ENGLISH-LANGUAGE TERMINOLOGY

In use (advocacy communities differ):
Disabled people
People with disabilities
People with [_____ diagnosis] (exception: Autistic rather than "with Autism")
Accessible [bathroom, parking, etc.]

Out-of-date:
Handicapped [person]
Handicapped [bathroom, parking, etc.]

When in doubt, avoid words that have been used as a slur or taunt (unless you clarify that you are describing a historical context in which they were medically "correct"). Some words have been reclaimed (e.g., from the stigmatized word *cripple*, disability activists claim the shortened form *crip* as a term of pride). Similarly, words that are often used with little connection to the actual original disability-related meaning may be tossed about with little or no intent to insult disabled people, and yet, reinscribe the perception of a particular kind of disability as a negative trait (e.g., *lame*, *retarded*).

Many disability self-advocates are critical of terms that seem to avoid the word disability or gloss over it "nicely" – (the #SayTheWord campaign seeks to disarm the ableist assumption that the word *disability* is always *bad* by simply using the word itself):

Differently abled
Handi-capable
Special/special needs
(and many more)

Disability advocates also track and disdain phrases in general usage that imply an ableist perspective:

Confined to a wheelchair (as activists counter that wheelchair use is
    an experience of increased freedom and mobility, not confinement)
Suffering from [X diagnosis]
(and many more)

For longer lists, and further reading see:
AUCD Resources on Portrayal of People with Disabilities
Ableist Words and Terms to Avoid, by Lydia X.Z. Brown
The National Center on Disability and Journalism "Disability
    Language Style Guide"

Russian-Language Terminology

The word used for "disability" in Russian most frequently is *invalid (een-vawl-LEED)* or *invalidi (een-vawl-LEED-dee)* in the plu-
ral. Note that while the spelling is the same, the pronunciation is
quite different from the English world "invalid." While both words
share a common derivation, the designation of a honorable war
wounded soldier in eighteenth century German, the meanings of
"invalid" in English and *invalid* in Russian are quite divergent.
While in English the word "invalid" signifies a somewhat archaic
description of one who is sickly, harkening a sort of nineteenth century vocabulary of ailment and convalescence, in Russian the range
of uses of the word *invalid* is quite similar to the way that disability
is used in contemporary English. For instance, a state pension for
a long term chronic illness or significant impairment is known as a
disability pension (or benefits) in English, and as a pension for *in-
validnost'*, the condition of being an *invalid*, in Russian. Also, while
the English speaker reads the Latin roots of invalid as characteriz-
ing the described person as "in-valid" or not valid, these latinate
root meanings are unfamiliar to Russians, and so the word invalid
is in fact perhaps less directly indicative of a lack or shortcoming
than the English dis-ability. Throughout the play, the characters
sometimes use the word *invalid* or *invalidi* to talk about disability.
When they do so, it can be delivered with the ease and disinterest
of an English-speaking person comfortable with the category *disability* using that word.

In Sergei's monologue, we see Sergei grappling with the com-
monplace word *invalid*, and consciously deciding to replace it with
the phrase *lyudi s invalidnostu*, or people with disabilities. *Lyudi s
invalidnostu* is a phrase that disability advocates began using around
2006–10 to follow the transnational trend of "people first language"
(see above).

Much like in English, there is a wide range of disability-related
vocabulary in Russian, ranging from medical and legal terminology for specific diagnoses (*nevrologicheskoe rasstroistvo, narusheniye
zreniya*), to complex journalistic and governmental language derived
from transnational human rights discourse (*lyudi s invalidnostu, bez*

bariernaia sreda, deti s autismom), to ableist slurs tossed about by playground bullies and internet trolls (*debil, dauni, bolvan*). Few of these words and phrases appear in the English language script of the play, but many were used in the course of the source interview material.

Appendix 3: Russian and Soviet Historical References

LIST OF POLITICAL LEADERS OF RUSSIA AND THE SOVIET UNION[1]

1613–1917 – The Romanov Dynasty rules the Russian Empire.

1917 – Overthrow of the Tsar; Provisional Government of Russia established; Bolsheviks triumph over Mensheviks, calling for Communism rather than democratic rule; Russian Civil War.

1917–24 – **Vladimir Lenin**, leader of the Bolsheviks, and, subsequently, first leader of the Soviet Union.

1924–53 – **Joseph Stalin** is the most notorious of Soviet leaders. His leadership carried the USSR from a revolutionary polity organized according to Leninist principles into the military power that made up a major component of allied forces in World War II, defending against the invading Nazi army. Russians today recall his status as a great leader and his harsh authoritarianism and punishing punitive measures that sent citizens and POWs to their deaths at harsh labor camps.

---

1 The dates of the various leaders' terms here are drawn from a simple reference encyclopedia entry for the purpose of offering readers of this volume or performers of the play not familiar with Soviet history a quick point of reference; naturally, historians will have more detailed takes on the particulars of leadership. "Leaders of Muscovy, Russia, the Russian Empire, and the Soviet Union" (2018), *Encyclopedia Britannica*, accessed 22 December 2018, https://www.britannica.com/topic/Leaders-of-Muscovy-Russia-the-Russian-Empire-and-the-Soviet-Union-1832695.

1953–64 – Nikita Khrushev led the Soviet Union in the post-war years, as the Cold War tensions emerged between the USSR and Europe and the US.

1964–82 – Leonid Brezhnev is widely considered by contemporary Russians to have been the best leader of the Soviet Union, and indeed of Russia in living memory.[2] During his leadership, citizens in Russia enjoyed relative comfort and absence of repressive force when compared with the strife of earlier eras of Soviet life (in spite of economic stagnation). His leadership is not recalled so fondly in Eastern Europe and Soviet satellite states. Most remarkably, Brezhnev himself became disabled by a stroke while in office. As Alina and her mother remark in the play, his assistants and handlers were seen to support him as he walked. In one photo, the ailing leader is depicted swimming in Crimea wearing an inflation device.[3]

1982–4 – Yury Andropov, previously the head of the KGB (the State Security Committee of the Soviet Union), won the support of the Communist Party to lead the Soviet Union after the death of Leonid Brezhnev in 1982. However, Andropov too died in office, leading for only 15 months.

1984–5 – Konstantin Chernenko Like Andropov, Chernenko is rarely discussed in general conversation. He led the Soviet Union for only a few months beginning in March 1984, and died in office in March 1985. He had been a close confidant of Brezhnev.

1985–91 – Mikhail Gorbachev, last leader of the Soviet Union, architect of Glasnost' who opened the Soveit system to internal democratic reforms and foreign cultural exchange.

1991–9 – Boris Yeltsin, President of the Russian Soviet Federative Socialist Republic (RSFSR) of the Soviet Union, Yeltsin became a hero as a major player in thwarting an attempted military coup of the Soviet Union, and was subsequently elected the first president of

---

2   For a useful English-language overview of a popular opinion survey of Russians by the Levada Center around the time when this play takes place, see RT from 22 May 2013, "Russians Name Brezhnev Best Twentieth-Century Leader, Gorbachev Worst," accessed 22 December 2018, https://on.rt.com/o930s3. The original Levada Center report was posted publicly in 2011 and titled "*Epokhi v zhini strani: Yeltsin, Gorbachev, Brezhnev* (Epochs in the life of the country: Yeltsin, Gorbachev, Brezhnev)," accessed 22 December 2018, https://www.levada.ru/2011/01/25/epohi-v-zhizni-strany-eltsin-gorbachev-brezhnev/.

3   I thank Anastasia Kayiatos for introducing me to this image.

the Russian Federation, the new nation state established roughly on the territory of the RSFSR in 1991.

1999–2008 – Vladimir Putin – Putin's first two terms as president were marked by a stabilization of Russian political and economic life in the post-Soviet era. On the international stage, the global war on terror offered Putin language to posture alliances with the US, and to pursue a brutal war at home against Islamic separatists in Chechnya.

2008–12 – Dmitry Medvedev – Medvedev, a member of Putin's United Russia party, was often considered during his time in office to be a more beneficent leader than Putin, offering more fanfare around internal humanitarian policy. Yet, Russians made fun of his short stature and dorky dancing, considering him a dupe, and Putin, who remained prime minister, to be the one really in charge, as the grip of the United Russia party on politics throughout all of Russia tightened. But, following Medvedev's single term in office (he himself seemed surprised when Putin announced that he would run for president again, interpreting the constitution's wording to mean that a president could not serve more than two *consecutive* terms) his corrupt schemes to embezzle state funds for lavish mansions and a personal vineyard were exposed by opposition activist Alexei Navalny, forever shifting public opinion of Medvedev.

2012–present – Vladimir Putin – In spite of high profile popular protests against Putin's new term, Putin's return to the presidency was marked by a profound reconsolidation of power, and the expulsion of foreign government and nonprofit organizations from the country. In 2014, Russia's annexation of Eastern Ukraine, along with the involvement of both Russia and the US in the Syrian civil war, led to a renewed era of animosity on the global stage between Russia and the US, and deepening nationalism at home.

Suggestions for Further Reading in Soviet History

Hosking, Geoffery. 2012. *Russian History: A Very Short Introduction.* Oxford: Oxford University Press.

Seventeen Moments in Soviet History (scholarly web resource with historical primary source material). http://soviethistory.msu.edu/.

Suny, Ronald Grigor. 1998. *The Soviet Experiment.* Oxford: Oxford University Press.

IN RELATION TO DISABILITY IN SOVIET HISTORY

Galmarini-Kabala, Maria Cristina. 2016. *The Right to Be Helped: Deviance, Entitlement, and the Soviet Moral Order*. DeKalb, IL: Northern Illinois University Press.

McCagg, William O., and Lewis Siegelbaum. (1989) 2009. *The Disabled in the Soviet Union: Past and Present, Theory and Practice*. Pittsburgh: University of Pittsburgh Press.

Phillips, Sarah. 2011. *Disability and Mobile Citizenship in Postsocialist Ukraine*. Bloomington: Indiana University Press.

Rasell, Michael, and Elena Iarskaia-Smirnova, eds. 2013. *Disability in Eastern Europe and the Former Soviet Union: History, Policy and Everyday Life*. New York: Routledge.

Shaw, Claire L. 2017. *Deaf in the USSR: Marginality, Community, and Soviet Identity, 1917–1991*. Ithaca, NY: Cornell University Press.

Appendix 4: Suggestions for Reading This Book in the Classroom

This book has many elements, and those who wish to bring the work to life in the classroom may wonder where to start.

The play itself may be read simply as a text – much as one would read a collected volume of oral histories. This is particularly useful if you are interested in reading the work for life history content, as an example of lived experience in Russia.

However, as I've argued in the ethnographer's essay, performance does things that text alone cannot. I urge instructors to consider devoting a class period to performing sections of the script.

Below is a suggestion of how you might run such a class, assuming that students would have read at least the script itself (or a section of the script) in advance. Depending on the subject matter and the level of the course, you might also assign the full ethnographer's essay, or parts of the ethnographer's essay (e.g., only section 3 for an undergraduate anthropology class; the full essay, with instructions to focus on the "making of" sections for a methods course; the background section and the section on representing Russia for an area studies course; the introduction, section 3, and the second "making of" section for a disability studies course, etc).

> First, divide students into groups of three, and give each group a scene to rehearse, with the assignment to have one person play the main role, one person play any peripheral roles, and

one person read the scene description and stage directions. Each group should take 30–40 minutes to (a) rehearse their scene, giving one another feedback about how to perform the parts, and (b) discussing collaboratively how they would stage the scene. What props would they absolutely need? What kind of set and scenery would they like to have, and what is absolutely necessary to convey the meaning of the scene? What blocking, beyond the stage directions, might they add? They should make use of the appendices to help with pronunciation, prop lists, and historical context. Each group should do a cold reading of their entire monologue, performing quietly to one another, and stopping to discuss issues as they go, then pick a five-minute excerpt (roughly one-third of a given monologue) to perform for the larger group. Be sure to give plenty of time to rehearsal – this is fundamental to the process. Depending on the number of students in the course, you may have multiple groups workshopping the same scene.

Next, bring the whole group back together. Depending on your students, you may meet resistance when it comes to performing in front of the larger group, so it's best to just insist on going in order through the script. If you decide to take multiple class periods to do this, you might rehearse one day and then perform another day; or if you have a longer class block, you could choose to perform the full 90-minute play. If you have multiple groups with the same monologue, you can decide if they should be allowed to elect one group to represent that monologue, or, if you have time, perform multiple renditions of the same scene – this will draw out contrasts in terms of how two different groups interpret the same scene.

Finally, following the performances, discuss. Ask the students to discuss their process. What did they find difficult, surprising, easy, fun, or unexpected about rehearsing their scene? Was there anything that they understood when reading the script aloud or attempting to embody the characters that they hadn't considered when they were just reading the text? Was there anything that they understood differently from watching each other's performances? What remains uncertain or hard to understand? Engaging in this work of rehearsing and performing the script collaboratively will generate many questions about interpretation. What is meant by this line? What emotional tone will be best for delivering a particular line? Encourage disagreements, and reflections on when and why disagreements may have emerged in the rehearsal process. What would you need to know or learn about in order to resolve the disagreements? Naturally, discussion topics and emphasis will vary depending on the topic and level of the course.

You might also assign exercises from Appendix 1, either as in-class activities or as homework. For a performance ethnography course in which students are developing their own performance works, it may be appropriate to assign several of the exercises spread over several weeks, interspersed with other readings in performance ethnography. For an anthropology methods course in which students are working through their own material, you might offer students the opportunity to pick one of the exercises (e.g., Exercises 2, 3, or 4) to do as a homework assignment, and then have them share the products with one another during class.

Of course, the best scenario is to stage or attend a production of the play, either in full or as an excerpt. Following along in the text while watching or listening to a recorded performance can work for a segment of the play. For information about accessing recordings of past performances, please contact the playwright, or visit the companion website to this book, www.iwasneveralone.org.

Appendix 5: Prop and Set List

Scene 1: Vera

- Wheelchair (manual)
- Table with table cloth suitable for a café
- Two chairs (café)
- Napkin holder with **paper napkins** (café)
- Salt and pepper shakers (café)
- Two large menus
- Flip phone with a bedazzled or glittery case
- Tea cup and saucer
- **Teapot with tea**
- Small plate
- Fork, knife, and teaspoon
- **Sugar cubes** in a serving bowl
- **Pastry (e.g., a fruit-filled strudel, croissant, or similar)**
- Other café props and furnishings according to the scene description and production needs

Scene 2: Vakas

- Rolling desk chair
- Desk
- Computer with mouse (desktop)

- Stationary bicycle
- Other room furnishings according to the scene description and production needs

Scene 3: Alina

- Wheelchair (manual)
- Computer with mouse (desktop)
- Desk
- Couch
- Shelf
- Newspaper or TV guide
- Komsomol card
- Old photo
- Other room furnishings according to the scene description and production needs

Scene 4: Sergei

- Plastic bag
- Stool
- Slippers
- Coat rack
- Table (apartment kitchen)
- Two chairs
- Two teacups, saucers, teaspoons
- Sugar bowl
- **Teapot with tea**
- **Wafer cookies in packaging**
- Flip phone (plain silver or black with a silence button on the side)
- Other room furnishings according to the scene description and production needs

Scene 5: Rudak

- Wheelchair (manual)
- Café tables and chairs
- Guitar and other instrument cases

- Microphone cords and audio cables
- Amplifier
- Other room furnishings according to the scene description and production needs

Scene 6: Anya

- Wheelchair (motorized power chair)
- Table (apartment kitchen)
- **Clementines** in a bowl
- Loose grocery store bakery **cookies** in clear plastic bag
- Flip phone on a lanyard
- Rubber gloves (e.g., for household cleaning)
- Plastic cup (reusable, but made from light plastic)
- **Pitcher of water**
- **Unwrapped bendable drinking straw**
- Other room furnishings according to the scene description and production needs

Consumables

- **Teapot with tea**
- **Sugar cubes** in a serving bowl
- **Pastry (e.g., a fruit-filled strudel, croissant, or similar)**
- **Wafer cookies in packaging**
- **Clementines** in a bowl
- **Loose grocery store bakery cookies** in clear plastic bag
- **Pitcher of water**

Appendix 6: Dramaturgical Note

STAGING ETHNOGRAPHY

Ethnography is a genre of qualitative social research that depends on long-term fieldwork that facilitates social relationships and draws on open-ended interviews and analysis of those interviews as well as observational fieldnotes.

Returning to this central element of the script can carry forward a great many of the dramatic decisions that directors and actors will make as they bring the text into space.

CASTING

When possible, actors with disabilities should be cast in the main roles. Emphasis in casting should be on artistic match with the role, and the disability of the character need not "match" the "real life" disability of the performer.

Theaters should anticipate that casting actors with disabilities may take time, longer than casting nondisabled actors. Nondisabled actors playing the main roles may benefit from conversations with paid consultants who have experience living with disabilities similar to those of their characters. At the same time, please remember that many disabilities are invisible, and in casting and discussing the disability status of a cast, one may not know whether actors participating in the project consider themselves to be disabled, and disclosing disability information is a personal choice.

Media: Audio Tracks, Music, and Digital Projections

An original musical score with a theme for each character was composed by Vladimir Rudak especially for this work, and may be played in transitions between scenes, and/or as walk-in music.

Ambient audio in Russian may be played as walk-in or fade-in, and tracks prepared from the source material interviews are available for use.

The online correspondences, text messages, and digital videos that occur throughout the text may be projected, sent to audience members' own devices, or displayed in some way.

Consider offering audiences a Russophone version of the script of the play in print or in digital format for viewing on personal devices with a link listed in the program.

Please contact the playwright if you are interested in using a media package composed of any or all of these elements in your production.

THEATER ACCESS

Directors may take the production of this work as an excuse to review the accessibility of their own theater.

I urge organizers to collaborate with local disabled self-advocates, inviting people with disabilities to act as advisors to the production, or help to workshop scenes with the actors. Please make it a practice to pay consultants on disability access issues for their unique expertise, and to take the time to locate consultants who are themselves members of the disability community.

On the most basic level, some of the following should be taken into consideration: simultaneous text transcription in English and/ or ASL interpretation, audio description of the action for the visually impaired, a neurodiversity-friendly option, and wheelchair seating with appropriate sightlines and access to exits and restrooms will facilitate an accessible experience. Full or excerpted elements of the scene description at the start of each portrait may be read aloud.

But more important is to think about accessible theater as a process of negotiating relations, rather than as a commitment to meeting standards on a checklist; this means starting from thinking of accessibility as an artistic choice that shapes the aesthetic of the play (for a further discussion, see Appendix 7, and the section of this book titled Casting and Rehearsing Access).

Appendix 7: An Ethic of Accommodation by Terry Galloway, Donna Marie Nudd, and Carrie Sandahl

1 At its core, an Ethic of Accommodation means that the majority does not rule. Instead, accommodation means including everyone wanting to participate, often necessitating that the majority make[s] difficult changes in its practices and environment. These changes are not made begrudgingly, but with goodwill, creativity, and a strong dose of humor, elements that often find expression in the performances themselves.

2 The ethic includes the politics of listening as well as the politics of speaking. Whereas most minority groups maintain that they have been "silence" by the majority and thus place speaking at a premium, disability communities often place listening on the same plane. People with disabilities often feel they have not been listened to or even addressed. In this context, listening does not have to happen with the ears. Listening, here, means to be taken into consideration, being attended to.

3 The Ethic of Accommodation means making room for difference possible, letting go of preconceived notions of perfectability, and negotiating complex sets of needs. Often these "needs" compete with one another. Accommodating disability or other forms of difference often does not seem practical or marketable, since doing so often raises costs or necessitates work that seemingly benefits only a few. Marketability is not our concern.

4 The Ethic of Accommodation inspires creative aesthetic choices
from casting, choreography and costuming, and also the sue of
space for the creation of new material. Practicing the ethic enhances
theatrical practice. (Galloway, Nudd, and Sandahl 2007, 229)

Appendix 8: Russian Words and Pronunciation

NOTES ON PRONUNCIATION

Russians roll the letter R, similar to in Spanish. The letter "H" in Russian, usually transcribed as "kh" is a guttural sound, like the Hebrew "ch" in "challah."

Unstressed consonants at the end of words are "devoiced": hot dok, instead of hot dog, and at the beginning of words (Vs turn into Fs).

Overall, Russians speak without opening the mouth very wide, and especially compared to American English speakers, hardly move their jaw at all as they speak. As a result, sounds are formed by moving the lips and the tongue, while the jaw is held in a steady position with the teeth just slightly parted. This, combined with the grammatical imperative to drop the pitch of a phrase to indicate the end of a sentence are what given English speakers the impression that Russians speak in a low voice. In fact, many Russian women use a very high voice.

Russian Words by Scene

VERA

v koliaske [vVff-kol-YAWs-kyeh] – in a wheelchair
Chto budete? [Sh-TOE BOO-dyeh-tyeh] – What'll ya have?
invalidi [een-vawl-LEED-dee] – disabled people, the disabled

Svetlana [Sveat-LAHN-nah] – woman's first name (option to add a typical Russian patronymic, e.g., Svetlana Mikhailovna, here for authenticity)

Igor [EE-gore] – masculine first name. In Russian the stress is on the first syllable, which is pronounced as a long "e" sound, not as an "I"

Andrei [awn-DRAY] – masculine first name, rhymes with "tray"

babushka [BAH-boosh-kah] – grandmother, grandma (if stressed on the middle instead of first syllable, you pronounce a different word, ba-BOOSH-kah, which means kerchief)

Da [daw, or dah, or short duh(!)] – the word for yes, but pronounced with all the variation in length, stress, and meaning that English speakers put into variations like Yep, or Yeah, or on occasion, well, actually. Also a common way to answer the phone when you know who is calling, e.g., Yes, dear? or, Hi Igor.

Chechnya [cheh-ch-nYUH] – separatist region in southwest Russia where Russian enlisted men were sent; similar to saying that someone was in Afghanistan/Iraq in the US context. In Russian the "nya" is pronounced as a single syllable.

Vsyo Idial! [VIS-yo EE-dee-ahl] – Everything is perfect!

VAKAS

Olga [OHL-gah] – feminine first name. In Russian it sounds quite sweet: start the word as if starting to say the English word "old."

"VK" or VKontakte – Russian social network similar to Facebook

ALINA

Tyotyenka [TYO-tien-kah] – Auntie

Mashkov [mash-KOVE] – a celebrity's last name – e.g., Vladimir Mashkov is the Tom Cruise of Russia

sil [SEEL] – strength, frequently in a moral, rather than physical, sense

Komsomol – a common Soviet word for the All-Soviet Communist Youth Organization

Medvedev [MYED-vyed-dyev] – the third president of the Russian Federation (after the collapse of the Soviet Union) served from 2008 to 2012, between Putin's second and third terms (the constitution prohibits more than two consecutive terms). Dmitry Medvedev did not run for a second term himself, but was appointed prime minister by Putin in 2012. Currently the prime minister as of this writing. Boyish and generally perceived to be more liberal than Putin.

Brezhnev [BREZH-nyev] – leader of the Soviet Union (General Secretary of the Central Committee of the Communist Party of the Soviet Union), 1964–82. Brezhnev died in office and was widely known to be very ill for the final years of his service of Gen Sec: images of a frail and aging Leonid Brezhnev are a popular joke on the Russian internet. Recognizable to Westerners as The One with the Bushy Eyebrows.

Gorbachev [gor-bah-CHYoff] – Mikhail Gorbachev, the last leader of the Soviet Union, 1985–91, he was Gen Sec of the Soviet Communist Party until 1990, then the President of the Soviet Union until its dissolution until 1991. Recognizable to Westerners as The One with the Birth Mark on His Head.

Ufa [oo-FAH] – a city in central Russia

Sergeich – the stage name of the comedian, it is the short version of a masculine patronymic, the kind of moniker that male classmates might call one another casually, teasingly, affectionately

Pavel Volia [PAH-vell VOWL-yeh] – man's first and last name. Comedian and MC of the popular TV show she is discussing.

Oporniki [oh-POUR-knee-kee] – medical term for a category of disability, people with impairments of motor-movement

SERGEI

Da – Yes

internat [een-TEAR-knot] – boarding school, esp. a boarding school for children with disabilities

Perezhivau eksperimenty! [pear-reh-ZHEE-vai-you ehk-spair-ree-MYEHN-tee] – I am always surviving experiments!

Zabolevaniye [zah-bowl-leh-VAWN-knee-yeh] – affliction, impairment

The Letter to Eugene *Onegin [Oh-NYE-gen]* – famous novel in verse, by Pushkin, adapted as an opera and in various other performative genres

Stidno [STEED-no] – embarrassing

Nedobovialis' [knee-dough-baw-VAH-lease] – unfriended, lit. un-added (e.g., to a list of friends on a social media site)

Kheppi Endink [KHEP-ee ANH-dink] or *Kheppi End [KHEP-ee ANHd]* – Happy Ending. A phrase, like Happy Birthday, that spoken in English with a thick accent permeates Russophone conversations (though nearly unintelligible as English).

RUDAK

Volodienka [Vuh-LOH-dyen-kah] – the most diminutive form of Rudak's first name, Volodya (i.e., his pal is joking by calling him the name a mother might affectionately use for a four year old child)

MNE?! [min-YEH?!] – To me?!?

Rossiya!! [roh-SEE-yah] – Russia (the name of the country/homeland in Russian)

ANYA

Vospriyatiye [vos-pre-YAH-tee-yeh] – upbringing; how someone is raised or educated, esp. with a moral/social connotation

Tak [TOK] – So …

Pit' budesh'? [PEET BOO-dyesh?] – Do you want something to drink?

yeshyo [Ye-SHOW?] – More?

Nyet, spasibo.[NYET, spah-SEE-bah] – No, thank you

Khorosho [khore-ROW-shuh] – Okay; that's fine; sounds good

Louhi [LOW-oo-khee] – rural region in Northern Karelia

Alekseevna [al-lek-SYAY-yev-nah] – feminine patronymic, used with a first name in formal address, e.g., instead of Mrs. So-and-so, Russians would say So-and-so Patronymic

Teaching Culture
UTP Ethnographies for the Classroom

Editor: John Barker, University of British Columbia

This series is an essential resource for instructors searching for ethnographic case studies that are contemporary, engaging, provocative, and created specifically with undergraduate students in mind. Written with clarity and personal warmth, books in the series introduce students to the core methods and orienting frameworks of ethnographic research and provide a compelling entry point to some of the most urgent issues faced by people around the globe today.

Recent Books in the Series:

Printed and bound by CPI Group (UK) Ltd, Croydon, CR0 4YY

13/04/2025

14656521-0001